Neighborhood Influences on Health among Black ar

by

Lea Raye Bromell

Department of Psychology & Neuroscience
Duke University

Date:_____

Approved:

_____
Keith E. Whitfield, Co-chair

_____
Linda M. Burton, Co-chair

_____
Philip R. Costanzo

_____
Laura S. Richman

A dissertation submitted in partial fulfillment of the
requirements for the degree of Doctor of
Philosophy in the Department of Psychology & Neuroscience
in the Graduate School of
Duke University

2011

UMI Number: 3452929

All rights reserved

INFORMATION TO ALL USERS
The quality of this reproduction is dependent upon the quality of the copy submitted.

In the unlikely event that the author did not send a complete manuscript
and there are missing pages, these will be noted. Also, if material had to be removed,
a note will indicate the deletion.

UMI®
Dissertation Publishing

UMI 3452929
Copyright 2011 by ProQuest LLC.
All rights reserved. This edition of the work is protected against
unauthorized copying under Title 17, United States Code.

ProQuest®

ProQuest LLC
789 East Eisenhower Parkway
P.O. Box 1346
Ann Arbor, MI 48106-1346

ABSTRACT

Neighborhood Influences on Health among Black and White Adults

by

Lea Raye Bromell

Department of Psychology & Neuroscience
Duke University

Date:_____

Approved:

_____
Keith E. Whitfield, Co-chair

_____
Linda M. Burton, Co-chair

_____
Philip R. Costanzo

_____
Laura S. Richman

An abstract of a dissertation submitted in partial
fulfillment of the requirements for the degree of Doctor of
Philosophy in the Department of Psychology & Neuroscience
in the Graduate School of
Duke University

2011

Copyright by
Lea Raye Bromell
2011

Abstract

The current study examined the relationships among neighborhood environment, self-efficacy, health behaviors, and health outcomes among adults in the United States. The goals of the research were to: 1. examine the role that health behaviors play in the relationship between neighborhood and health; 2. determine whether health-related self-efficacy mediates or moderates the relationship between neighborhood and health behaviors; and 3. investigate potential gender, education, and race differences in the relationships among the constructs.

The study included 5,600 whites and 321 blacks who participated in the first wave of the National Survey of Midlife Development in the Unites States (MIDUS I). The age range of the sample was 20-75 (mean= 47.14 years) and roughly half of the participants were male (47.4%). Data on neighborhoods (including safety, physical conditions, social cohesion, and homeplace) and health self-efficacy, behaviors, and outcomes (e.g., self-rated health, obesity, and cardiovascular disease) were collected through telephone interviews and self-report questionnaires.

Data analysis was conducted using structural equation modeling. Results indicated that self-efficacy mediated the relationship between neighborhood and physical activity and that health behaviors mediated the path between neighborhood and physical activity. However, self-efficacy did not serve as a moderator in the association between neighborhood and physical activity. Demographic differences were found according to age, gender, race, and education. Specifically, the model was particularly salient for late midlife and older adults, females, and those with some college education. Furthermore, the impact of neighborhood factors on self-efficacy was greater for blacks than whites.

The present findings contribute to the literature by elucidating the interrelations among neighborhood and the individual-level factors of self-efficacy and physical activity in predicting health outcomes. Furthermore, the direct effect of physical activity on health outcomes suggests that physical activity engagement should be a particular area of intervention focus, especially among older adults and women. Future research should include objective measures of neighborhood, physical activity, and health, additional contexts such as the workplace, individuals above the age of 75, and greater representation of minority groups.

Table of Contents

Abstract..	iv
List of Tables...	x
List of Figures...	xi
Acknowledgements..	xii
1. Introduction..	1
2. Literature Background...	3
Adult Development and Aging as an Area of Inquiry......	3
Definitions of Age Periods within Adulthood..............	3
Why is Adulthood an Increasingly Vital Area of Study?.....	5
Adult Health in the United States..	7
The Current Picture of Health in the U.S. Adult Population.	7
Self-rated Health..	8
Cardiovascular Disease.................................	9
Obesity...	9
Health Disparities in the United States...................	10
Disparities by Age.......................................	10
Gender Disparities......................................	10
Disparities between Blacks and Whites.....................	11
Underlying Mechanisms of Health Disparities..........	11
Theoretical Background Linking the Person and Environment.........	14
Person/Gene-Environment Interactions & Correlations........	14
The Ecological Framework of Human Development............	16

Lawton's Ecological Theory of Aging..................................	17
Conceptual Models of Neighborhood, Health, and Aging................	18
The Causal Model of Neighborhood Effects on Aging.........	18
The Conceptual Models of the Current Work.......................	21
Neighborhood & Homeplace as Developmental Contexts...............	23
Neighborhood as a Developmental Context.................................	23
Rates of Exposure to the Neighborhood Environment...................................	24
The Neighborhood as a Social Arena........................	25
Individuals' Cognitive & Physical Decline...............	26
Homeplace as a Developmental Context..............................	26
Empirical Links between Neighborhood & Homeplace Factors and Health...	28
Safety...	28
Physical Conditions...	30
Social Cohesion...	32
Homeplace...	34
Adaptive/Maladaptive Health Behaviors..	35
Smoking..	36
Physical Activity..	38
Personal Competencies: The Case of Self-Efficacy........................	41
Definition and Theory of Self-Efficacy................................	42
Evidence of the Link between Self-Efficacy and Health Behaviors..	44
3. Research Questions & Hypotheses..	46

4. Methods...	47
The National Survey of Midlife Development in the United States (MIDUS)...	47
Participants..	47
Data Collection...	48
Sample & Measures of the Current Study..	49
Participants..	49
Measures..	50
Neighborhood & Homeplace Factors.........................	50
Self-Efficacy..	51
Health Behaviors..	52
Health..	53
5. Statistical Analysis..	54
Descriptive Statistics..	54
Structural Equation Modeling...	54
Estimation...	54
Evaluation of Model Fit..	55
SEM Analysis Step 1: The Measurement Model...................	56
SEM Analysis Step 2: Structural Model 1............................	58
SEM Analysis Step 3: Structural Model 2............................	59
SEM Analysis Step 4: Testing Demographic Differences....	59
6. Results..	60
Descriptive Statistics..	60
Correlations...	64

Indicator Correlations with Demographic Variables.............	64
Correlations of Indicators within Latent Constructs.............	65
Correlations across Indicators of Latent Constructs.............	66
Structural Equation Modeling Results................................	69
Confirmatory Factor Analysis..................................	69
Structural Model 1...	70
Structural Model 2...	74
Demographic Differences in Structural Model 1..................	75
7. Discussion..	80
The Latent Factors: Included and Excluded Variables......................	80
Structural Model 1 Fit the Data...	82
Self-efficacy Did Not Moderate the Neighborhood-Physical Activity Relationship...	86
Demographic Differences Were Evident in Model 1.......................	86
The Model Was Particularly Salient for Late Midlife and Older Adults..	86
Greater Impacts Were Found for Females...........................	89
The Influence of Neighborhood on Self-efficacy Was Greater for Blacks...	91
Education...	91
Limitations...	93
8. Conclusion..	96
References..	99
Biography..	118

List of Tables

Table 1. Demographic Characteristics of the Study Participants (N=5921)........... 50

Table 2. Descriptive Statistics, Correlations with Demographic Variables, and Correlations with Other Indicators of Latent Variables for 18 Indicators of Latent Variables.. 62

List of Figures

Figure 1. M. Powell Lawton's ecological model of aging... 18

Figure 2. The causal model of neighborhood effects on aging (Glass & Balfour, 2003). 19

Figure 3. Conceptual model of hypothesized relations (Model 1).................................. 22

Figure 4. Conceptual model of hypothesized relations (Model 2).................................. 22

Figure 5. The measurement model... 57

Figure 6. SEM results for structural model 1.. 72

Acknowledgements

I first and foremost thank God for strength, peace, joy, and love- without which nothing would be possible! Thank You, Lord, also for blessing me with amazing opportunities and individuals throughout my life- a few of whom I would also like to take the time to acknowledge.

I wish to thank my dissertation committee for their help, encouragement, and support throughout my graduate career. A very special, heartfelt thank you to Keith Whitfield and Linda Burton for being dedicated advisors before even officially beginning the role. The many conversations about remaining in the process when I had decided to end early were invaluable. Your commitment to my success is one of the primary reasons I have achieved this accomplishment- thank you for not allowing me to settle for less!

I would like to additionally thank you, Keith Whitfield, for mastering the art of exceptional mentorship. You truly found the perfect balance between keeping me on track, allowing my independence, and just laughing and having fun- I couldn't ask for more. The things that I have learned from you in the last few years, from professional tips to old school phrases, will continue to shape my growth.

Thank you again, Linda Burton. Linda, you are my inspiration! I am constantly amazed by your scientific rigor, overall wisdom, and personal grace. Thank you for having faith in me and knowing exactly how to guide me through not only this process, but also life's many polishing moments.

Thank you, Philip Costanzo, for sharing your many insights and demonstrating what it means to be a well-versed and accomplished scholar.

Thank you, Laura Richman, for pushing me with your thoughtful questions, your dedication to good science, and flexibility in helping me stay on course.

I would like to also thank you, Dr. Chongming Yang, for your invaluable expertise and assistance in performing the Mplus analyses. You are a statistical rockstar!

Thank you to all of the faculty, staff, and fellow students in the Duke University Psychology & Neuroscience department. It takes a village to raise a Ph.D. and I couldn't have asked for a better academic family.

A very special thank you to Nancy Hill- without you I would have never started this journey. Thank you for the countless times you were there for me both professionally and personally- they will not be forgotten.

To my wonderful friends- many thanks, you are all priceless! I wish to give special thanks to Monique Faulk. Monique, how do I even begin to thank you for your friendship and all you have done for me? You truly are the greatest bff- thank you for always reminding me of what's important and helping me remain focused on the plan. Jochebed Gayles, thank you for being the fabulous you, our many conversations that taught me a lot about my future goals, and the countless memories that still make me laugh. To Jennifer White- thank you for 15 years of ridiculous laughter and fun. You are the epitome of a lifelong friend and I appreciate your constant reminder of who I've always been. Hayley Mitchell, thank you for Dissertation Fridays, lunch dates, my $0 gig (and many similar raises), but most of all for welcoming me into your awesome family for so many memorable holidays. To Naomi Jean-Baptiste- you are a genuine friend. I would like to thank you for sincerely celebrating my milestones and inspiring me with all that can be accomplished with true dedication. Thank you, Ashleigh Hales, for waterfall dates during the rough patches and the lovely Lauren Dallas Hales, who brightened up the last few months of writing. Most importantly, thanks to all of my friends for so many YAY moments!!

Last but not least, thank you to my entire family. Especially, thank you to my beautiful sisters, Jana, Tai, and Morgen- you are the best! Nothing was more motivating than the example and support of my favorite women. Thank you to my brothers, Bryon and Matt, for loyally giving your time and energy. I wish to give a big-hug-sized thank you to my parents for believing in me from day 1 (literally) and providing me with the tools to come this far. I am eternally grateful for the many ways you raised this little girl into a woman.

1. Introduction

As life expectancy and the median age of the United States population are on the rise, the study of adulthood and aging is becoming increasingly relevant to our society. Although people are living longer, significant declines in health associated with aging remain. For example, self-rated health status has been demonstrated to decline and cardiovascular disease to increase with age. Other health indicators show more of an inverted U-shaped pattern, such as obesity, which is at its highest levels in late midlife and then decreases in later life. To some extent, health declines are expected with age; however, health behaviors also impact individuals' health trajectories across adulthood. The most influential of these behaviors are physical activity, a health-promoting behavior, and smoking, a health risk behavior. These factors are significantly influenced by the context in which individuals live. Furthermore, theory and research suggest that the environment, including characteristics of the neighborhood context, plays a critical role in individuals' health. While research on the interrelations among the environment, individual factors, and health has shown marked increases over time, the processes through which the person and environment interact to effect health have not been fully elucidated.

The aim of the present dissertation is to further contribute to the person-environment literature on aging. The goals of this work include: 1. To examine the relationships among the neighborhood context and individual characteristics that impact health; 2. To determine whether differences in the person-neighborhood interaction are apparent with aging; 3. To test potential gender, ethnicity, and education differences in health based on the relationship between the context and the individual.

The present work is organized as follows. In the first section, an extensive review of the relevant *Literature Background* on aging, health, and neighborhood is outlined. Based on the theory and empirical work examined, *Research Questions and Hypotheses* are posed. A description of the National Survey of Midlife Development in the United States (MIDUS) study as well as the specific participants and measures utilized in the current study are presented in the *Methods* section. Based on the hypotheses and research questions, the *Statistical Analysis* plan is provided followed by the *Results* of these analyses. Finally, a *Discussion* of how the findings relate to the previous literature, the real-world significance of the findings, study limitations, and future directions completes the current work.

2. Literature Background

Within this review of the relevant literature, the importance of examining adult development and aging will first be discussed. Second, using national data, health status and trends within the U.S. adult population, including health disparities along age, gender, and ethnicity, will be highlighted. Third, the theoretical background of person-environment relations as well as the conceptual models that will serve as the framework for the analyses will be presented. The neighborhood and homeplace environments will then be considered in terms of their role as developmental contexts, with a particular focus on adult development and aging. Next, the empirical evidence on the impact of neighborhood and homeplace factors on adult health will be presented. Then, the health behaviors of smoking and physical activity will be taken into account. The review will conclude with an investigation of individuals' self-efficacy, followed by an integration of the literature reviewed.

Adult Development and Aging as an Area of Inquiry

Research within the field of developmental psychology often focuses on infants, children, and adolescents. While a great deal of development occurs during these life stages, it continues beyond the early years as adults are also developing agents. However, there is less focus on adult development and aging in the literature on development. Given this, the current section will discuss the definitions of age periods within adulthood that are adopted in the present work as well as the compelling issues of adult research.

Definitions of Age Periods within Adulthood

The age at which one becomes an adult varies by culture and historical time period. Currently, within the United States, one is legally considered an adult at age 18, as evidenced by legal rights such as those to work, vote, marry, and join the military without parental consent. In the current paper, the period of young adulthood is characterized as the age range of 18-34. While discrete age periods are difficult to operationalize, previous research suggests that biological functioning and physical performance wane after 35 (Shephard, 1998), demonstrating a meaningful developmental difference in terms of health trajectories at this age.

The developmental stage of middle adulthood is difficult to define due to individual variation in life paths, changing demographics, increased life expectancy, and differing views across cultures (Lachman & James, 1997; Moen & Wethington, 1999). Furthermore, there is debate over whether midlife is best defined by chronological age or life events, statuses, and roles (Lachman & James, 1997; Merrill & Verbruggee, 1999; Moen & Wethington, 1999). The latter definition may result in a life stage of less variation; however, given the highly variable experiences of adults, it may also exclude members on alternate paths who identify as middle adults. Given this consideration, it is posited that chronological age is a more inclusive and preferable marker of middle adulthood.

In terms of population-based conceptualizations of middle age, younger individuals tend to report a younger range (those in their 20s report midlife as ages 30-55 years) than older individuals (those in their 60s and 70s report midlife as ages 40-70 years); however, across adults, the typical midlife range reported is 35-65 years (Lachman & James, 1997; Lachman, Lewkowicz, Marcus, & Peng, 1994). In order to encompass the typical spectrum of those who identify as midlifers and because this age range has also been supported by experts in the field of middle adulthood (Willis & Reid, 1999), I define middle age as 35-65 years. Given the large range of ages and the expected developmental differences between those at either end of the range, there is utility in further dividing the conceptualization of middle adulthood into early midlife (35-50 years) and late midlife (51-65 years). Not only does this split equally divide the period of middle adulthood, it is also relevant to physical development. For example, the median age of the start of menopause is reported to be between 50 and 52 years old (Avis, 1999).

Generally speaking, older adulthood is widely accepted as ages above 65 years old. This may be partly due to the fact that 65 years old was the age of retirement within the United States for many years (although the full retirement age is gradually increasing, as it is currently 66 years old and expected to reach 67 years old by 2027) (Office of the Chief Actuary, 2009; Social Security Online, 2009). Although some researchers have further divided older adulthood into categories such as young-old, middle-old, and old-old or oldest-old (Atchley, 2000; Fisher, 1993; Kolb, 2008), the current work does not make these distinctions within older adulthood.

Why is Adulthood an Increasingly Vital Area of Study?

The study of adulthood and aging is becoming increasingly relevant to our aging society. Due to factors such as advances in medicine, declines in health destructive behaviors, and lower death rates, adult health and life expectancy have both shown improvements over time (Ferraro, 2006; Kolb, 2008). The "baby boomers" (those born between 1946 and 1964) (United States Census Bureau, 2006), one of the largest birth cohorts in the history of the United States, are currently in midlife (with some soon entering late life). For these reasons, the median age of the population is increasing. In 1990, the median age in the U.S. was 33 years; however, the projected median age for 2050 is 42 years (Willis & Reid, 1999). In terms of adults aged 65 and older, it is projected that the number of non-Hispanic whites will double and the number of blacks will more than triple by 2050 (Angel & Hogan, 1992). The aging of our society demands an increase in research on adult development. Furthermore, the characteristics and roles of adults within the United States also provide compelling support for this research; these are discussed below.

The period of young adulthood is considered a particularly complex and challenging one that is characterized by increasing variability across individuals' life paths (Konstam, 2007; Tanner & Yabiku, 1999). This developmental stage is a time of instability (including the exit of familiar settings such as the home and school), exploration (especially in the areas of love and work), responsibility, and optimism (Arnett, 2006; Konstam, 2007). Given the diversity of experiences within young adulthood and the large implications that this period has for the remaining adult stages and possible future paths, young adulthood is a critical research area for developmental psychology.

Those in middle adulthood (as defined above) are considered by some to be the most productive people in society in terms of work/career (as the most employed individuals as well as those earning the highest income levels), power and influence (as the most likely to be civic and economic leaders), family (as those most often caring for children/adolescents and/or elderly adults), and community (as a large portion of those involved in local community service) (Neugarten, 1968; Willis & Martin, 2005; Willis & Reid, 1999). Within developmental psychology, the research on middle adults often focuses on the parental role and how parents impact their children's development (see, Ryff & Seltzer, 1996). However, these adults' own development, which will inevitably influence their parenting, is less researched. This results in a gap in the literature not only on adult development, but also on parenting and family.

Older adulthood is the stage of greatest declines, particularly in the physical (e.g., increases in frailty and chronic diseases), cognitive (e.g., decreases in memory and fluid intelligence), and social arenas (e.g., deaths of family and friends) (though it is important to note that there is great variability in losses across individuals), as well as some gains, such as in knowledge, expertise, and wisdom (Baltes & Smith, 1990; Kolb, 2008; Settersten Jr., 2006). The burdens of the losses, particularly those related to disease and disability, experienced during this life stage on the individual, family, society, and economy are substantial (for example, see Geldmacher, 2009; Raskind, Bonner, & Peskind, 2004). Therefore, research on older adulthood, particularly that which may identify or lead to the decrease of losses, stabilization, or the increase of gains, is necessary to limit these burdens and promote successful aging.

Adult Health in the United States

Throughout much of the history of the United States, health was conceptualized as the absence of disease. However, in 1948, the World Health Organization re-defined health as a "state of complete physical, mental, and social well-being and not merely the absence of disease or infirmity" (WHO, 1948). This broader and more inclusive definition has been widely adopted in both theory and research application and is adopted in the present work.

The Current Picture of Health in the U.S. Adult Population

While there are a multitude of health indicators, the current paper focuses on a subset of important factors (i.e., self-rated health, cardiovascular disease, and obesity). Self-rated health has consistently been classified as a useful indicator of individuals' perceptions of their overall health status (Fayers & Sprangers, 2002). Of the chronic conditions, cardiovascular disease is the most prevalent. In fact, it is the leading cause of death in the United States (Heron, et al., 2009). In the U.S., obesity is one of the fastest growing (in prevalence) conditions that is associated with a variety of negative health consequences (Flegal, 2005; National Center for Health Statistics, 2008). For these reasons, self-rated health, cardiovascular disease, and obesity are the health variables of interest in the present study. A deeper examination of each of these health indicators, including recent U.S. statistics, follows.

Self-rated Health. Self-rated health is individuals' subjective perception of their health. In measurement, individuals are typically asked to rate their "health", "physical health", and/or "mental health". Self-rated health is a reliable predictor of mortality, morbidity, and health behaviors (Fayers & Sprangers, 2002; Idler & Angel, 1990; Idler & Benyamini, 1997; Idler, Russell, & Davis, 2000; Malmstrom, Sundquist, & Johansson, 1999; Mossey & Shapiro, 1982), and has been shown to have greater predictive power than physician-rated health (Idler & Angel, 1990; Mossey & Shapiro, 1982). Furthermore, the relation between self-rated health and mortality has been found for both men and women as well as for all of the major ethnic groups found within the United

States (McGee, Liao, Cao, & Cooper, 1999). U.S. data from 2006 demonstrates that 9.2% of the population's subjective health status was fair or poor (it should be noted that this value includes individuals under the age of 18; however, specific rates for adults are provided by age group in the section on health disparities with age) (National Center for Health Statistics, 2009).

Cardiovascular Disease. Cardiovascular disease refers to a class of diseases that involve the heart or blood vessels (see for example, Maton, 1993). As previously mentioned, it is the leading cause of mortality in the United States. A national survey, conducted in 2007, found that 11.2% of the adult (18+ years) population had heart disease (including coronary heart disease, angina pectoris, heart attack, or any other heart condition or disease) and 23.2% were hypertensive (defined as being told that they had hypertension or high blood pressure on two or more doctor visits) (Pleis & Lucas, 2009).

Obesity. Obesity is measured by Body Mass Index (BMI), which is calculated by taking individuals' weight in kilograms and dividing it by their height in meters squared. Among adults, obesity is defined as a BMI greater than or equal to 30 kilograms/meter^2. Obesity is a risk factor for multiple diseases such as cardiovascular disease, diabetes, hyperlipidemia, and some cancers (Black & Macinko, 2008; Flegal, 2005), with the condition associated with high medical costs (Daviglus, et al., 2004; Flegal, 2005). Data trends have shown steadily increasing obesity rates over time among U.S. adults (Flegal, 2005; National Center for Health Statistics, 2008, 2009). For the 2003-2006 period, 33.4% of adults 20 years and over were classified as obese (National Center for Health Statistics, 2009), with the prevalence of obesity doubling since 1980 (Flegal, 2005; National Center for Health Statistics, 2008).

These statistics show the health of the general population of the United States; however, disparities are evident based on age, gender, and race/ethnicity. A breakdown of these disparities as well as a brief discussion of the possible mechanisms underlying the disparities, as posited by researchers, follows.

Health Disparities in the United States

Disparities by Age. National data demonstrates that self-rated health status declined with age (percent of persons with fair or poor health: 18-24 years: 3.7%; 25-44 years: 6.3%; 45-54 years: 12.9%; 55-64 years: 18.8%; 65 years and over: 24.8%) (National Center for Health Statistics, 2009), whereas cardiovascular disease increased with age (Pleis & Lucas, 2009). Of the age groups, those in late midlife (55-64 years old) demonstrated the highest levels of obesity (males: 39.3%; females: 41.0%), with decreases observed in later life (National Center for Health Statistics, 2009).

Gender Disparities. The life expectancy of females is greater than that of males. In 2006, females' life expectancy was approximately five years greater than that of males (80.2 years & 75.1 years, respectively) (Heron, et al., 2009). According to the most recent national statistics, rates were similar for males and females for the health measure of fair or poor self-rated health (males: 9.0%; females: 9.5%) (National Center for Health Statistics, 2009). In terms of obesity, a greater percentage of females (35.2%) is affected than males (33.1%) (National Center for Health Statistics, 2009). However, both heart disease (males: 12.5%; females: 10.2%) and hypertension (males: 23.3%; females: 22.9%) were experienced by a greater percentage of men than women, though the difference in hypertension was small (Pleis & Lucas, 2009).

Disparities between Blacks and Whites. For most causes of death, blacks have the highest mortality (Adler, 2006, 2009; Dressler, Oths, & Gravlee, 2005; Heron, et al., 2009). Furthermore, blacks' life expectancy has consistently been found to be less than that of whites (see, for example, Bulatao & Anderson, 2004). For example, the life expectancy of blacks was five years less than that of whites in 2006 (73.2 years & 78.2 years, respectively) (Heron, et al., 2009). For most of the health indicators of interest to the work described here, blacks demonstrated a health disadvantage. A greater percentage of blacks identified as having fair or poor health as compared to whites (14.4% vs. 8.6%, respectively) (National Center for Health Statistics, 2009). An ethnic comparison by gender shows that while a similar percentage of white and black females had heart disease (10.6% and 10.5%, respectively), a greater percentage of white males were classified as having heart disease (13.4%) than were black males (9.6%). Even though white males experience a greater degree of heart disease, blacks are more likely to die from heart disease than are whites (Davis, Vinci, Okwuosa, Chase, & Huang, 2007; Mensah & Brown, 2007). Furthermore, blacks were more likely to be hypertensive (black females: 34.5% vs. white females: 21.6%; black males: 28.7% vs. white males: 23.4%) (Pleis & Lucas, 2009). Ethnic differences in obesity are apparent, especially among females. A greater percentage of black males (35.7%) are obese as compared to white males (32.4%). However, there is a stark difference between black and white females, with over half of black females (53.4%) measured as obese compared to 31.6% of white females (National Center for Health Statistics, 2009).

Underlying Mechanisms of Health Disparities. Various underlying mechanisms have been considered in the health disparity literature. These can be broadly categorized as biological, structural, psychosocial, and behavioral mechanisms. For the most part, health decline over time is an expected condition of biological aging. However, biological/genetic models of gender and ethnic differences in health outcomes have received little support (Dressler, et al., 2005; Whitfield, Weidner, Clark, & Anderson, 2002); therefore, the current review focuses on structural, psychosocial, and behavioral mechanisms of health disparities.

Structural mechanisms include factors such as financial differences and differential medical treatment, and may be particularly relevant in the consideration of age and ethnic disparities. Older individuals and ethnic minorities are more likely to experience financial difficulties related to health, health care, and health insurance, which may then lead to limited access to good health care, medications, and other treatments (Auchincloss, Van Nostrand, & Ronsaville, 2001; Davis, et al., 2007). Furthermore, "the accumulation of effects associated with disadvantage leads to increasing disparities over the life course, with the largest differences seen in middle and late adulthood" (Adler, 2009, p. 665), demonstrating another avenue by which financial structure causes disparities with aging. Differential medical treatment could be impacted by these financial differences; however, there is also some evidence that ethnic minorities receive differential treatment at nearly every level of diagnosis, care, and prevention even when financial barriers are taken into account (see for example, Davis, et al., 2007).

Health disparities may also arise as a result of differences in psychosocial factors such as social support, depression, hostility/anger, stress, coping styles, and perceived discrimination/racism (see the following reviews, Adler, 2009; Brondolo, Rieppi, Kelly, & Gerin, 2003; Dressler, et al., 2005; Whitfield, et al., 2002; Williams & Mohammed,

2009). For example, women score lower on hostility, receive more social support from a larger number of sources, and while they are more likely to experience depression, they are also more likely to employ adaptive coping strategies (Whitfield, et al., 2002). As an example of ethnic/racial disparities, perceived discrimination/racism as well as stress (whether from perceived racism, exposure to high-stress environments, or other stressors) have been linked to health outcomes among African Americans (Brondolo, et al., 2003; Dressler, et al., 2005; Richman, Bennett, Pek, Siegler, & Williams Jr., 2007; Williams & Mohammed, 2009), which may impact the differences found between blacks and whites.

Behavioral factors may also contribute to health disparities. The most consistent finding in terms of behavioral differences with age is the decrease in physical activity. In terms of gender, men are more likely to participate in physical activities; however, they are also more likely to smoke, consume excessive amounts of alcohol, and have a poorer diet (see for example, Whitfield, et al., 2002). This might point to a female advantage in terms of the impact of health behavior on health. Ethnic differences in health behaviors have also been found. For example, African Americans experience the greatest health burdens from smoking, are less likely to engage in physical activity than whites, and are more likely to participate in risky sexual behaviors and contract sexually transmitted diseases (see for example, Whitfield, et al., 2002).

Thus far, the current work has considered the individual factors of age, gender, ethnicity, health, and health behaviors. However, individuals' development does not occur within a vacuum; the individual and environment interact in dynamic and complex ways throughout the lifespan. Therefore, theory on the relationship between the person and environment is presented as a starting point for the present work on neighborhood effects on health.

Theoretical Background Linking the Person and Environment

The nature vs. nurture debate was highly controversial in the early twentieth century; however, by the 1930s, attention began to shift to interactions between the person and the environment (Anastasi, 1958; Schwesinger, 1933) as a way of explaining individual variability in behavior. In Anastasi's (1958) influential paper, heredity and environment were conceptualized as intertwined such that heredity set the limits for the environment's impact on development. The author further stated that the relative contribution of heredity on a given trait is reliant on the environment and vice versa such that their contributions cannot be teased apart. These principals have been incorporated into and elaborated upon in subsequent considerations of the relationship between the individual and the environment. A review of the major person-environment theories, concluding with the theory and conceptual model that serve as a basis for the current work follows.

Person/Gene-Environment Interactions & Correlations

Similar to Anastasi's (1958) work, many prominent person-environment theories focus on the biology of individuals. This is evident in probabilistic epigenesis (Gottlieb, 1998, 2000) and developmental contextualism (Lerner, 1993). Probabilistic epigenesist is a gene-environment theory that claims that genes alone do not produce features of the individual; rather, genes are only able to express themselves appropriately in response to input that is external (including the physical, social, and cultural environment) and internal (including behavior, neural activity, and hormones) (Gottlieb, 1998, 2000).

Developmental contextualism, as posited by Lerner (1993), also describes the interaction between genes and environment. Here, genes and environment are considered of equal importance in individual development. In concordance with probabilistic epigenesist, developmental contextualism specifies that gene functioning is always reliant on the environment. Moreover, this theory further characterizes the environment as exerting a variable amount or type of influence on development depending on the biological makeup of those residing in the environment. Expanding upon Anastasi's (1958) conceptualization of heredity as limit-setting for environmental impacts on development, developmental contextualism claims that the interaction between genes and environment limits development to several potential pathways. These theories are useful to the present discussion in that they stress the importance of both person and environment variables; however, a greater consideration of aspects of the individual beyond genes as well as the varieties and processes of interaction is necessary.

The theory of person-environment interactions and correlations, as discussed by Rutter and associates (1997), classifies categories of relationships between the person and the environment. Person-environment interactions refer to the realization of an outcome due to an individual's susceptibility in conjunction with exposure to a specific environmental experience. Passive person-environment correlations represent the influence that parents' genes exert on a child through parenting and other environmental factors that parents provide their children. On the other hand, evocative person-environment correlations occur when the characteristics of an individual influences the ways in which others respond to that individual. Finally, individuals also seek out particular environments and experiences that may be correlated with their genotype, termed active person-environment correlations. This theory adds to the person-environment literature by characterizing methods through which the environment impacts individuals as well as through which the individual exerts an influence on the environment. However, a more comprehensive view of the environmental arena with which these interactions and correlations occur is lacking; this is provided in the ecological framework of human development.

The Ecological Framework of Human Development

The ecological framework emphasizes the interaction between the individual and multiple levels of the environment (Bronfenbrenner, 1977, 1979, 1989). Within this model, the individual has his/her own unique set of characteristics including biological, personality, and cognitive factors. Furthermore, the context is separated into several categories (microsystem, mesosystem, exosystem, macrosystem, and chronosystem) based on the relationship to the individual. The *microsystem* includes the individual's immediate environment; those settings that contain the individual. Interactions among these microsystems compose the *mesosystem*, which includes, for example, home-neighborhood interactions. The *exosystem* refers to environmental settings that do not contain the individual but impacts the individual's more immediate environment and, therefore, indirectly influences the individual. The overarching culture or subculture is termed the *macrosystem*, which includes aspects such as cultural customs and values, economic patterns, the culture of politics, and social conditions. Finally, development occurs through time and an individual's developmental history is represented by the *chronosystem*. While this theory considers various levels of the environment, it is best suited for considerations that look across all of these various systems. Therefore, a more specified theory of environment and aging, Lawton's ecological theory of aging, is considered.

Lawton's Ecological Theory of Aging

M. Powell Lawton's ecological theory of aging focuses on individuals', particularly adults', adaptation to the environment (Lawton, 1982; Lawton & Nahemow, 1973; Nahemow, 2000). Within this theory, the environment has four classifications: personal (i.e., significant social relationships), suprapersonal (i.e., model characteristics of those in close proximity), social (i.e., norms, values, and institutions), and physical (i.e., nonsocial features). These environmental systems exert press, or demands, on individuals. With time, individuals tend to adapt to the external environment, reaching their adaptation level (AL). However, individuals' ability and timing to reach their AL is impacted by their competence. Those with high levels of competence reach AL more quickly and are better equipped for stronger environmental press while those with low competence have a greater vulnerability to press. In general, older individuals often experience declines in various levels of competence and require a greater amount of time to reach AL. The interaction between environmental press and competence results in adaptive or maladaptive behavior. For example, those with low competence but strong environmental press are likely to exhibit maladaptive behavior. The interaction between environmental press and individual competence, and the resulting behavior, is depicted in the ecological model of aging (Figure 1). This theory and model are foundations for the study of person-environment relations in adulthood and aging. Given the broad scope of Lawton's theory, a more detailed consideration of how the interaction between the person and environment impacts health may aid in the conceptualization of the current work.

Such a model has been put forth by Glass and Balfour (2003). The current work utilizes this model as a base but slightly adapts it to models that more closely fit the research objective. These models are now discussed.

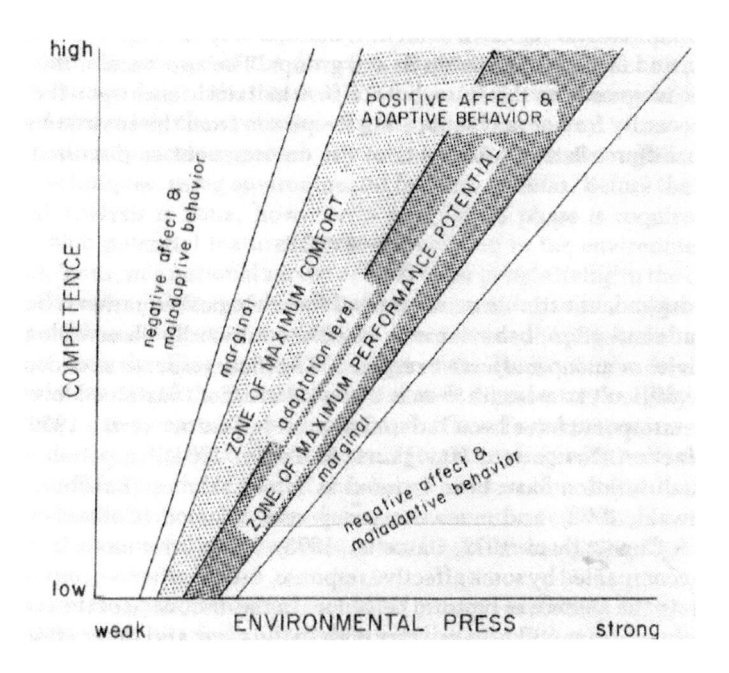

Figure 1. M. Powell Lawton's ecological model of aging

Conceptual Models of Neighborhood, Health, and Aging

The Causal Model of Neighborhood Effects on Aging

Thomas Glass and Jennifer Balfour's (2003) causal model of neighborhood effects on aging (Figure 2), an extension of Lawton's ecological model of aging, is employed as the base for the conceptual model of the present work on the relationship between the neighborhood and homeplace contexts and health. In short, neighborhood factors and characteristics serve as agents of buoying (defined as environmental factors that are beneficial for functioning) or press (defined as environmental demands); these then interact with individuals' competencies to determine the person-environment fit.

This balance between the person and environment then influences whether the individual will respond in an adaptive or maladaptive manner. Finally, these behavioral responses impact health and functioning; thus, expressing a multistep model of neighborhood effects on health. Now that the layout of the model has been presented, the various components that comprise it are discussed in greater detail.

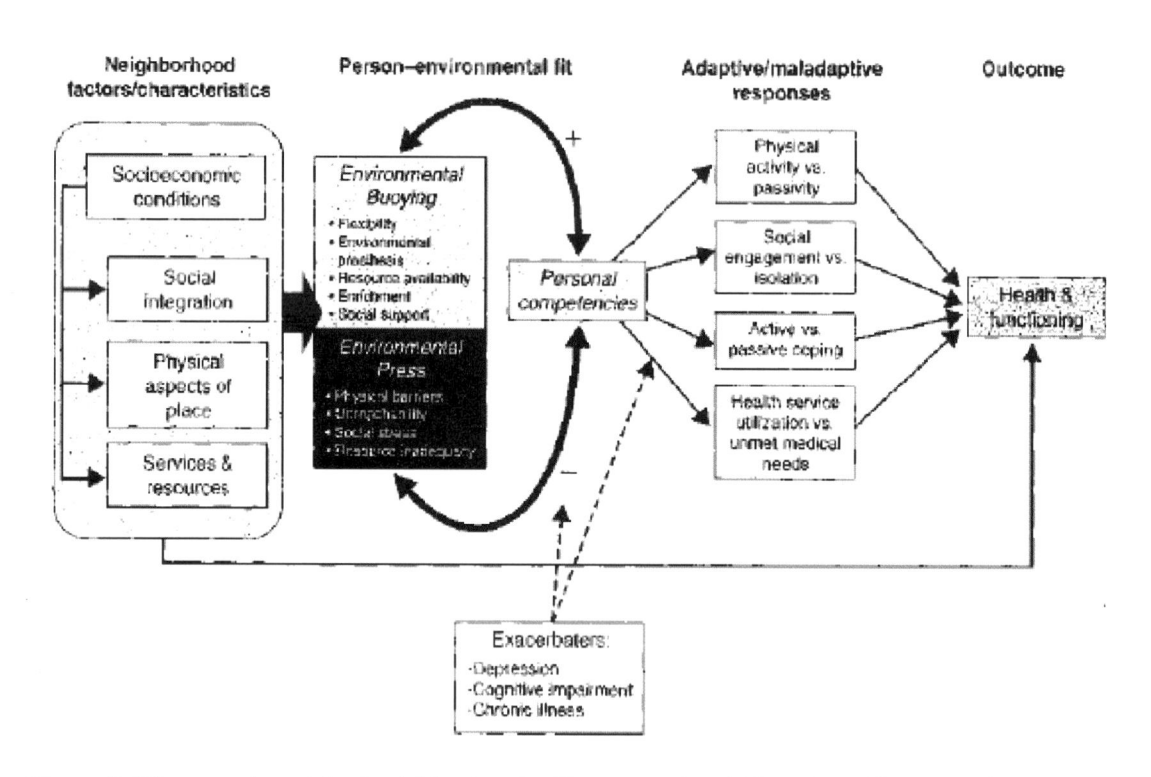

Figure 2. The causal model of neighborhood effects on aging (Glass & Balfour, 2003)

The conceptual model (Glass & Balfour, 2003) begins with consideration of neighborhood factors and characteristics. The creators of the model chose four dimensions as particularly influential in aging: socioeconomic conditions, neighborhood social integration, physical aspects of place, and services and resources. The variables of interest for the current study are captured in neighborhood social integration and physical aspects of place and, therefore, these features of the model are expanded upon. Social integration includes social cohesion, neighborhood safety and fear of crime, as well as aspects of homeplace. Physical aspects of the neighborhood include the conditions of the buildings, streets, sidewalks, etc. Social cohesion, safety, attachment to homeplace, and well maintained physical conditions may buoy or facilitate individuals' competence. On the other hand, a lack of these positive characteristics and the presence of negative features, such as those that instill a fear of crime, serve as environmental press or challenges. Both environmental buoying and press are hypothesized to influence older adults to a greater degree than younger adults.

The interaction between environmental buoying and press and personal competencies represent the person-environment fit. In their discussion of the model, Glass and Balfour (2003) focus on physical competencies and how an increase in limitations such as limited physical mobility results in an increase in the effect of environmental challenges. Likewise, a similar trend may be expected in other areas of competence such as self-efficacy. More specifically, lower levels of self-efficacy may heighten the effects of environmental press. Given that physical and cognitive declines may lower feelings of self-efficacy (Bandura, 1997), this is an especially important personal characteristic to consider within adult development and aging. The concept of self-efficacy and how it functions within the model will be further discussed later.

Person-environment fit then impacts individuals' behavioral responses. The authors (Glass & Balfour, 2003) discuss both the adaptive and maladaptive responses of four areas of behavior. These responses include physical activity vs. passivity, social engagement vs. isolation, active vs. passive coping, and health service utilization vs.

unmet medical needs. Given the current paper's focus on physical health behaviors, physical activity is considered and smoking behavior is added to the model. It is hypothesized that "if environmental press exceeds the individual's level of competence, then the resulting behavioral response may be maladaptive" (Glass & Balfour, 2003: 322). Thus, individuals experiencing greater environmental press and lower levels of self-efficacy, especially older adults, may be more likely to engage in maladaptive health behaviors. As may be expected, health behaviors then directly impact health outcomes. The causal model of neighborhood effects on aging serves as a starting point for the conceptual models designed for the present paper; these models will now be outlined.

The Conceptual Models of the Current Work

The first model that will be examined in this dissertation is depicted in Figure 3 (Model 1). In short, this model asserts that the relationship between neighborhood/homeplace and health is mediated by health behaviors. Additionally, the relationship between neighborhood/homeplace and health behaviors is mediated by self-efficacy. An alternate model is also proposed (Model 2; see Figure 4). Similar to the first model, the alternate model states that health behaviors mediate the relationship between neighborhood/homeplace and health. However, rather than self-efficacy serving as a mediator, self-efficacy serves as a moderator in the relationship between neighborhood/homeplace and health behaviors. A more detailed discussion of the models follows.

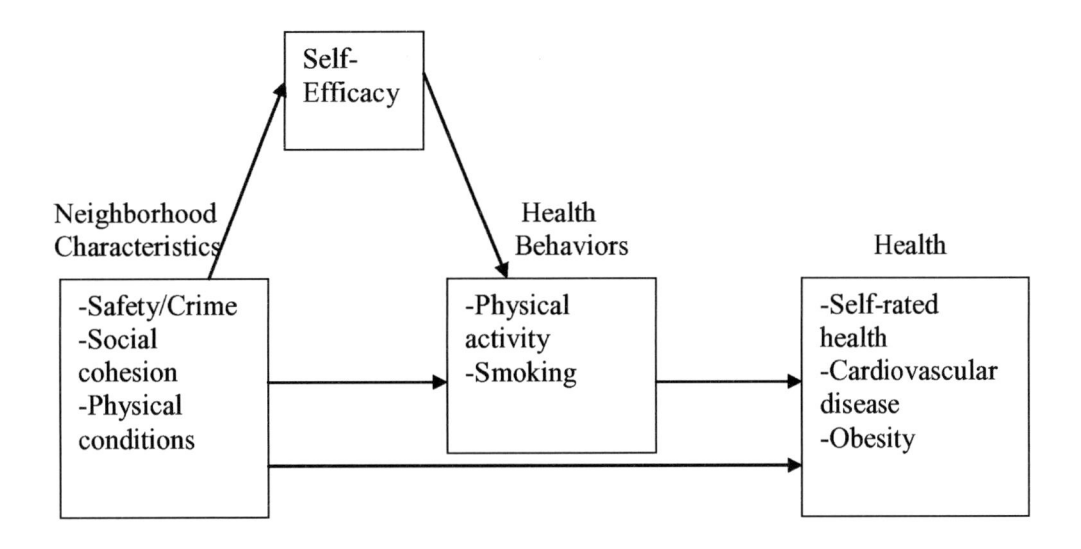

Figure 3. Conceptual model of hypothesized relations (Model 1)

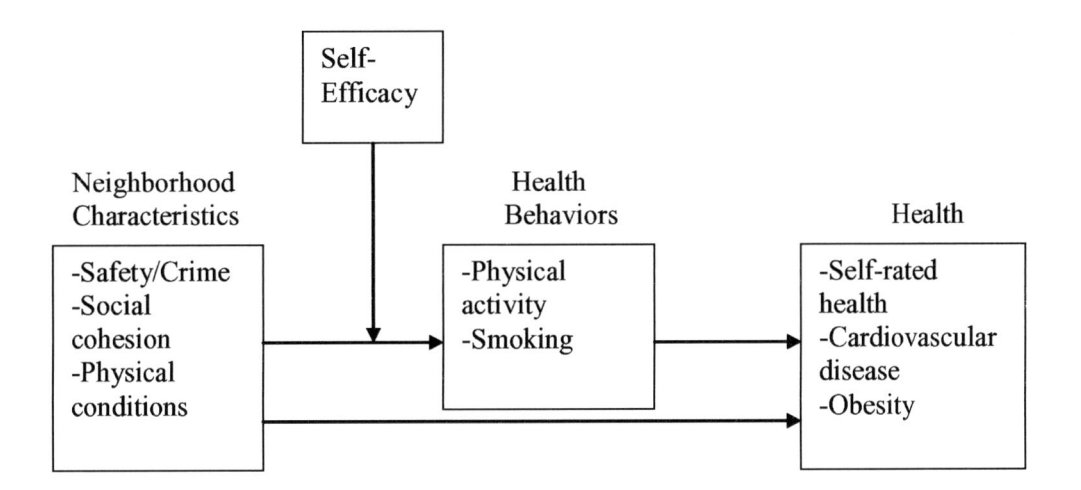

Figure 4. Conceptual model of hypothesized relations (Model 2)

Similar to Glass and Balfour's (2003) model, the current models (Figure 3 & 4) posit that neighborhood characteristics impact health. The models also incorporate person-environment fit and health behaviors. According to Glass and Balfour (2003), person-environment fit (the interaction between environmental press and buoying and personal competencies) influences adaptive/maladaptive behaviors in a path-like manner, and it is through this path that neighborhood exerts it effects on health. Although the current model also considers person-environment fit and health behaviors, these are represented in roles that differ from those shown in the causal model of neighborhood effects on aging. More specifically, health behaviors mediate the relationship between neighborhood characteristics and health. Person-environment fit remains in the model, but here personal competencies (i.e., self-efficacy) serve a mediating role in the relationship between the context and behaviors in the first model (Figure 3) and serve a moderating role in the relationship between context and health behaviors in the alternate model (Figure 4). As discussed above, the health outcomes that will be examined include self-rated health, cardiovascular disease, and obesity. Now, an in-depth view of the constructs that are proposed to impact these outcomes is provided, beginning with the contextual elements.

Neighborhood & Homeplace as Developmental Contexts

The neighborhood and homeplace environments serve as more than geographic locations within an individual's life. Development occurs within these contexts and the relationship with and impact of the environment may vary across age. Literature on the neighborhood and homeplace as developmental contexts for adults is reviewed.

Neighborhood as a Developmental Context

Within the field of developmental psychology, considerations of neighborhood as a developmental context have primarily focused on children and adolescents. In particular, neighbor affluence and neighborhood resources (e.g., child care, schools, medical facilities) have been examined in terms of children's cognitive, health, and socioemotional outcomes; social disorganization theory has been applied to problem behaviors among neighborhood youth; the indirect impact of neighborhood on child development through parenting behaviors has been researched (For a review, see Leventhal & Brooks-Gunn, 2000). As noted, neighborhood influences have been investigated among adults in terms of parenting within this field; however, the examination of adults as developing agents is limited. In order to comprehensively theorize about the neighborhood as a developmental context for adults, literature from sociology and epidemiology is integrated into the discussion. The rates of exposure to the neighborhood environment, neighborhood as a social arena, individuals' cognitive and physical decline, and homeplace as a developmental context are examined.

Rates of Exposure to the Neighborhood Environment. The meaning and experience of the neighborhood environment can be theorized to change as individuals age. First, rates of exposure, both in terms of daily life and duration, differ by age group (Cagney & Cornwell, in press; Glass & Balfour, 2003; Oh, 2003). While young and midlife adults tend to leave their neighborhood for a large portion of the day for work and recreational environments, many older adults remain embedded within the home and neighborhood throughout the day (Glass & Balfour, 2003; Krantz-Kent & Stewart, 2007; Oh, 2003; Robinson & Godbey, 1997). Furthermore, as a direct function of time and aging, older residents spend a greater duration of time in their neighborhood. This is especially true given that rates of residential mobility are low among the older adult population (Cagney & Cornwell, in press; Oh, 2003). The higher degree of exposure may suggest that the neighborhood has a larger impact on older adults as compared to their younger counterparts; however, the type of impact varies by neighborhood characteristics. For example, the length of residence in a neighborhood may positively affect relationships with neighbors, social cohesion and trust, and positive evaluations of and attachment to the neighborhood (Oh, 2003). However, if the neighborhood is an unhealthy environment, longer duration of exposure may result in negative developmental consequences (Glass & Balfour, 2003). As an example, neighborhood crime (and even fear of crime) and disorder weaken social bonds, cohesion, trust, and feelings of security, and older individuals may particularly withdraw from their neighbors and neighborhood as a result (Bursik Jr. & Grasmick, 1993; Liska & Warner, 1991; Oh, 2003; Ross & Mirowsky, 1999; Sampson & Raudenbush, 1999; Skogan, 1990; R. B. Taylor, 1996). As is evident from these examples, the neighborhood is not only a physical environment, but also a social arena. The developmental importance of the social aspects of the neighborhood is now discussed.

The Neighborhood as a Social Arena. In young and middle adulthood, life events such as marriage, having children, and participating in the workforce increase social networks and interactions (Hansson & Carpenter, 1994; Oh, 2003). However, social ties decline with age due to factors such as the deaths of family members and friends, exiting the workforce, and children moving from the parental house (Glass & Balfour, 2003; Kolb, 2008; Oh, 2003). Given these age-related changes, older adults tend to rely on the neighborhood as a source of social interaction to a greater degree than do younger adults (Glass & Balfour, 2003; Oh, 2003). Therefore, the social characteristics of the neighborhood may be expected to influence whether older adults are more likely to experience social isolation or social solidarity. Social ties with neighbors may also be especially vital in older age as cognitive and physical abilities decline; these changes are now discussed in relation to neighborhoods.

Individuals' Cognitive & Physical Decline. Older adults may undergo changes in their physical and cognitive abilities due to normative aging or diseases related to aging (it is important to note that there is a great deal of variability in changes in older adulthood, and capabilities in different domains may remain stable, decline, or improve) (Bandura, 1997; Kolb, 2008). Declines may cause older adults to be more vulnerable to maladaptive environmental conditions, experience lower levels of competence and self-efficacy, and withdraw from the social environment (Cagney & Cornwell, in press; Glass & Balfour, 2003; Oh, 2003). Negative neighborhood characteristics, such as crime, may exacerbate or even directly lead to these poor outcomes (Oh, 2003). On the other hand, positive neighborhood features such as social cohesion and trust may serve as protective factors. Although the neighborhood is a context for all human development, theory suggests that older adults may be more influenced by the neighborhood environment due to their greater exposure, increased reliance for social interaction, and physical and cognitive declines as compared to young and middle adults.

Homeplace as a Developmental Context

The concept of homeplace has been, for the most part, lacking from psychology. Therefore, literature from the fields of sociology, public health, and gerontology are utilized to shed light on its developmental significance. Burton and colleagues have defined homeplace as "a multilayered, nuanced family process anchored in a bounded geographic space that elicits feelings of empowerment, commitment, rootedness, ownership, safety, and renewal among family members" (Burton & Lawson Clark, 2005,

p. 166) (See also Burton, Win, Stevenson, & Lawson Clark, 2004). Carol Stack (1996), in her ethnography entitled *Call to Home: African Americans Reclaim the Rural South*, found that individuals often left the family homeplace in young adulthood and then returned in middle adulthood. It may be expected that middle adults who do not return to their childhood homeplace begin the process of creating a new homeplace. Both of these scenarios suggest that homeplace may have a greater meaning for and impact on midlife adults as compared to young adults. Furthermore, similar to neighborhood, a greater frequency of exposure heightens the attachment to homeplace (Shenk, Kuwahara, & Zablotsky, 2004). This implies that community-dwelling older adults may have a stronger attachment to homeplace as they are likely to have lived in and developed their homes for a longer duration than younger adults. As an example, the 2000 census found that approximately one-third of older adults resided in the same residence for at least 30 years (Cagney & Cornwell, in press). In addition, research indicates that older adults experience less fear about being alone in their homes than do younger adults (Jeffords, 1983), demonstrating a stronger sense of homeplace in terms of its role as a safe haven. Furthermore, the symbolic meanings of the home have been related to well-being and quality of life and may help to buffer against losses experienced due to aging (Fullilove & Fullilove III, 2000; Gitlin, 2003; Rubinstein, 1989). Overall, it appears as though homeplace increases in significance as a developmental context as individuals age.

In dealing with the association between developmental contexts and health, neighborhood level safety, physical conditions, and social cohesion as well as homeplace will be addressed in the present study. These features are of particular interest as they have each been theorized to impact adult health, especially among older adults. The question remains: do empirical investigations support these claims? The attention is now turned to a deeper discussion of these environmental features as well as empirical evidence of how these contextual factors impact adult health.

Empirical Links between Neighborhood & Homeplace Factors and Health

Safety, quality physical conditions, social cohesion, and homeplace have been labeled as important indicators of a healthy neighborhood (Macintyre & Ellaway, 2000; Macintyre, Ellaway, & Cummins, 2002b; S. E. Taylor, Repetti, & Seeman, 1997). Furthermore, these aspects of the neighborhood environment have shown empirical relations with the health outcomes of interest; these relations are discussed below.

Safety

The safety of a neighborhood is typically operationalized in terms of levels of crime and violence. While safety is a vital attribute of a healthy neighborhood, residing in an unsafe neighborhood may be expected to be detrimental to health. Objective and perceived levels of crime and violence have been linked to bodily harm, fear, stress, social isolation, and limited mobility within the neighborhood (Ferguson & Mindel, 2007; Macintyre, MacIver, & Sooman, 1993; Robert, 1998; Ross, 1993). Crime, violence, and safety have been empirically related to self-rated health (Chandola, 2001; Lindstrom Johnson, et al., 2009; Tucker-Seeley, Subramanian, Li, & Sorensen, 2009), cardiovascular disease (Black & Macinko, 2008; Chaix, Lindstrom, Rosvall, & Merlo, 2008; Franzini & Spears, 2003; Mobley, et al., 2006; Sundquist, et al., 2006), and obesity (Black & Macinko, 2008; Burdette, Wadden, & Whitaker, 2006; Mobley, et al., 2006).

In examining the influence of neighborhood violence on self-rated health, Lindstrom Johnson and colleagues (2009) recently conducted a study that assessed this relationship among 392 mothers residing in Baltimore City, Maryland. These women were primarily African American (94%) and most were between the ages of 20 and 29 (64%), with 17% under the age of 20 and 19% over the age of 30. Participants indicated their perceived safety and exposure to violence in the past 12 months. While perceived neighborhood safety was not significantly related to self-rated health, those who reported high exposure to neighborhood violence were nearly twice as likely to report poorer health.

A study in Sweden (Sundquist, et al., 2006) examined neighborhood violent crime and coronary heart disease among 336,295 men and 334,057 women between the ages of 35 and 64 years. Neighborhood violent crime was defined as violence against persons (e.g., homicide, robbery, rape) and this data was provided by law enforcement. For each neighborhood, the number of violent crimes was divided by the number of residents and the distribution was separated into quintiles. For both men and women, the risk of coronary heart disease increased as rates of neighborhood violent crime increased. This was particularly evident among those within the quintile with the highest levels of crime (odds ratio: 1.75 for women; 1.39 for men). In a smaller scale study of low-income women in the United States (Mobley, et al., 2006), crime (defined as the number of robbery arrests per 100,000 county residents) was positively associated with both coronary heart disease risk and body mass index.

In a study that investigated the relationship between safety and obesity, Burdette and colleagues (2006) surveyed 2,620 U.S. women (mean age 27.6 (±6.0) years). Levels of perceived neighborhood safety were measured as how often respondents witnessed social disorder such as gang activity, drug dealers, and disorderly groups. Results indicated that as levels of safety decreased, BMI values and the prevalence of obesity increased. While the abovementioned studies utilized different indicators of safety (e.g., perceived safety and disorder, exposure to violence, and objective crime statistics), they concur that neighborhood-level safety impacts health.

Physical Conditions

The physical conditions of the neighborhood include aspects such as cleanliness, the presence of graffiti, litter, and vacant or dilapidated buildings, aesthetic qualities such as greenery, and functional characteristics such as the presence and quality of sidewalks. In addition to the potential direct impact of the environment, poor physical conditions may decrease feelings of safety as the quality of the physical environment may either deter or promote criminal activity (e.g., the presence of vacant buildings may increase criminal activities such as drug dealing and prostitution) (Cagney & Cornwell, in press; Cohen, Mason, et al., 2003; Raudenbush, 2003; Skogan, 1990). Various neighborhood physical conditions have been related to the health outcomes of self-rated health (Cummins, Stafford, Macintyre, Marmot, & Ellaway, 2005; Ellaway, Macintyre, & Kearns, 2001; Franzini, Caughy, Spears, & Fernandez Esquer, 2005; Krause, 1996, 1998; Poortinga, 2006; Wen, Hawkley, & Cacioppo, 2006), cardiovascular disease (Cagney & Cornwell, in press; Cohen, Farley, & Mason, 2003), and obesity (Casey, et al., 2008; Ellaway, Macintyre, & Bonnefoy, 2005; Poortinga, 2006).

As shown, several studies have investigated the impact of physical conditions on self-rated health. Krause's (1996) paper includes a variety of environmental features and focuses on late life. A total of 931 U.S. adults 65 years of age and older (mean= 74.2 years, SD= 6.7 years) participated in the study. The physical neighborhood environment (labeled neighborhood deterioration in the study) was assessed by the interviewers (not the respondents) along the following six dimensions: condition of the interior of the respondent's dwelling, condition of the exterior of the respondent's dwelling, condition of other houses and buildings in the neighborhood, condition of the sidewalks and yards, the amount of noise, and the quality of the air. In order to examine self-rated health by differing levels of physical conditions, estimations were conducted for 1. one standard deviation below the mean deterioration value, 2. the mean score, 3. one standard deviation above the mean, 4. two standard deviations above the mean, and 5. the highest deterioration scores. Results show that health was not related to physical conditions among those in neighborhoods below and at the mean score. However, there was an incremental increase in the deleterious effect of poor physical conditions on health as these environmental conditions worsened, with the relationship particularly pronounced among older adults in neighborhoods with the highest deterioration scores.

Using U.S. Census data, Cohen and associates (2003) examined physical conditions of the neighborhood and premature death (defined as before the age of 65). The unit of analysis was 107 cities with populations over 150,000 and the measure of physical conditions used was the number of boarded-up units. This indicator of poor physical environment was moderately associated with premature mortality due to cardiovascular diseases. Although the unit of a city may be considered quite large to be labeled a neighborhood, the researchers conducted a similar investigation of 343 Chicago neighborhoods (defined through census tracts) and found a positive relation between the physical condition measure of "broken windows" (boarded up stores and homes, litter, and graffiti) and premature mortality due to cardiovascular disease (Cohen, Farley, et al.,

2003). In addition, using data from the National Social Life, Health, and Aging Project (NSHAP; a study of 3,005 community-dwelling adults aged 57-85), Cagney and Cornwell (in press) found that individuals who resided in poorly kept blocks (identified based on abandoned buildings, vandalism, litter, etc.) were more likely to suffer from hypertension. Combined, these studies demonstrate that poor physical conditions are positively related to chronic disease mortality.

To measure the impact of physical features on overweight and obesity, Ellaway, Macintyre, and Bonnefoy (2005) analyzed data from the Large Analysis and Review of European Housing and Health Status (LARES; n= 6,919 adults). In this study, trained surveyors rated the physical environment including the amount of graffiti, litter, and greenery surrounding the participants' homes. Individuals residing in areas with high levels of greenery were 40% less likely to be overweight or obese as compared to those with low levels of greenery. On the other hand, those in environments with high levels of graffiti and litter were 50% more likely to be overweight or obese. Similar to neighborhood safety, varying aspects of the neighborhood's physical conditions were measured in the studies presented; however, all point to a significant effect on physical health.

Social Cohesion

Social cohesion is defined in terms of neighbors' mutual trust, solidarity, connectedness, shared values, and support (affective and instrumental) (Kawachi & Berkman, 2000; Leventhal & Brooks-Gunn, 2000; Sampson, Morenoff, & Earls, 1999; Sampson, Raudenbush, & Earls, 1997). Neighborhoods that are socially cohesive may promote outdoor activities, access to services and amenities, and healthy behaviors through social norms and information as well as through the control of deviant behaviors, which may lead to heightened feelings of safety (Echeverria, Diez-Roux, Shea, Borrell, & Jackson, 2008; Franzini, et al., 2005; Kawachi & Berkman, 2000; McNeill, Wyrwich, Brownson, Clark, & Kreuter, 2006; Mendes de Leon, et al., 2009; Veenstra, 2000). Furthermore, individuals in socially cohesive neighborhoods are more likely to help and support each other (McNeill, et al., 2006), which may be particularly important for the health of older residents.

In terms of the physical health indicators of interest, social cohesion has been empirically shown to be related to self-rated health (Ellaway, et al., 2001; Kawachi, Kennedy, & Glass, 1999; Parkes & Kearns, 2006; Poortinga, 2006; Snelgrove, Pikhart, & Stafford, 2009) and cardiovascular disease (Chaix, et al., 2008; Kawachi, Kennedy, Lochner, & Prothrow-Stith, 1997); however, no empirical relations were found for obesity. A more detailed examination of a selection of this research follows.

In a recent study, Snelgrove and colleagues (2009) conducted a multilevel analysis of the relationship between social cohesion, defined as social trust, and self-rated health using the British Household Panel Survey (BHPS). The sample included 3,075 adults aged 16 and older who had complete information at baseline (wave 8; 1998) and follow-up (wave 13; 2003). Based on individual-level responses, the 250 postcode sectors represented by the sample were categorized as high trust areas (120; 48%) and low trust areas (130; 52%). The results demonstrated that residing in a high trust area reduced the odds of poor self-rated health, even after controlling for demographics, socioeconomic characteristics, and baseline self-reported health. In fact, the degree of the effect was such that the odds of poor health for those in low trust areas were similar to a 10-year age increase.

Considering the chronic disease of cardiovascular disease, a 39-state study was conducted using the General Social Survey of U.S. adults aged 18+ (Kawachi, et al., 1997). In this study, social cohesion was also calculated through levels of social trust. States with lower levels of social trust had higher rates of total and cause-specific mortality, including coronary heart disease mortality. Given that these results are based on state levels of cohesion, caution should be taken in narrowing the interpretation to the neighborhood level. However, an analysis of 7,791 individuals aged 45 and older in Sweden found that higher acute myocardial infarction mortality was associated with low neighborhood cohesion, even after adjusting for individual health, socioeconomic factors, and neighborhood confounders such as income and residential stability (Chaix, et al., 2008). This study demonstrates that neighborhood-level cohesion impacts chronic disease mortality.

Homeplace

Aspects of homeplace that are more often measured include attachment to place (in this case the place of residence) and homeownership. Of the environmental characteristics of interest, this is by far the least studied in terms of the health outcomes examined in the current work. Only two relevant studies were identified, one examined the relationship between homeownership and self-rated health and obesity (Poortinga, 2006) and the other identified homeownership as a factor relating to years of life lost to heart disease (Franzini & Spears, 2003). A more detailed consideration of these empirical works is now presented.

In the first mentioned study, Poortinga (2006) utilized data from the 2003 Health Survey for England (HSE). This data set includes 14,836 individual interviews with adults 16 years old and above within 720 postcode sectors. Homeownership was compared with renting, residing rent-free, and squatting. Findings demonstrated that those who owned their housing were less likely to be obese. Furthermore, those who did not own their dwelling were more likely to rate their health as poor. The second study (Franzini & Spears, 2003) examined heart disease deaths in Texas among those 25 years of age and over at time of death. Individuals' (n=54,640) addresses were geocoded to the census block-group, tract, and county. A higher percent of homeowners at the county level was negatively associated with years of life lost to heart disease (calculated based on the life expectancy at the age when death occurred).

The research discussed in this section indicates that each of the neighborhood and homeplace factors of interest is related to some or all of the health outcomes of self-rated health, cardiovascular disease, and obesity. However, there is a lack of research on potential underlying mechanisms of these relations. As suggested by Glass and Balfour's model (2003) as well as the conceptual models of the paper (Figure 3 & Figure 4), health behavior may serve an important mediating role. The health behaviors of smoking and physical activity are now discussed in terms of relation to disease, current trends in the U.S., and neighborhood and homeplace correlates.

Adaptive/Maladaptive Health Behaviors

The current paper adopts Steptoe and Wardle's (2004) definition of health risk behavior as "*any activity undertaken by people with a frequency or intensity that increases risk of disease or injury*" (pp. 25). Examples of health risk behavior include smoking, substance abuse, drunk driving, and unprotected sex with multiple partners. Given that cigarette smoking has been characterized as the health risk behavior with the greatest burden of disease and is related to heart disease as well as a multitude of other diseases (Centers for Disease Control and Prevention; Miles, 2006; Ross, 2000; Steptoe & Wardle, 2004), it is the health risk behavior of focus in the current work.

Health-promoting behaviors, on the other hand, are defined as "*activities that may help to prevent disease, detect disease and disability at any early stage, promote and enhance health, or protect from risk of injury*" (Steptoe & Wardle, 2004, pp. 25-26). These behaviors include participating in physical activity, maintaining a diet that is high in fruits and vegetables, using a seatbelt, and attending regular physician and dental visits. Of the various health-promoting behaviors, physical activity is the current focus as it has been conceptualized as that with the greatest health benefits and is strongly negatively related to obesity, cardiovascular disease, and a host of other diseases and conditions (Berlin & Colditz, 1990; International Agency for Research on Cancer, 2002; Katzmarzyk, Janssen, & Ardern, 2003; Pate, et al., 1995; Stein & Colditz, 2004; U.S. Department of Health and Human Services, 1996). The smoking and physical activity statuses of U.S. adults are now discussed along with the relation of these health behaviors with the neighborhood and homeplace contexts.

Smoking

The most recent national health data, from 2006, showed that 20.8% of adults aged 18 years and over were current cigarette smokers (defined as ever smoking 100 cigarettes in a lifetime and currently smoking every day or on some days) (National Center for Health Statistics, 2009). A greater percentage of men smoked as compared to women (23.6% vs. 18.1%, respectively), which has been a consistent pattern since cigarettes were introduced to the United States. In an examination of ethnic group differences by gender, black and white females exhibited similar percentages (18.8% and 18.5%, respectively) while a greater percentage of black males (26.1%), as compared to white males (23.5%), were current smokers. The age data show interesting midlife trends. Generally speaking, the percentage of smokers decreased with age for both the male and female population. However, while the white male population demonstrated the expected decrease from early midlife (25.3%) to late midlife (23.4%), a drastic increase was evident among black males (early midlife: 22.2% vs. late midlife: 32.6%). A similar, though less pronounced, trend was found among females (white early midlife: 21.7% vs. white late midlife: 18.8%; black early midlife: 21.0% vs. black late midlife: 25.5%). These data suggest that men and blacks (particularly those in late midlife) may experience a greater health disadvantage due to smoking behavior.

Each of the contextual variables of interest has been empirically related to smoking behavior. In addition to investigating the outcome variable of self-rated health, the Lindstrom Johnson and associates' (2009) previously mentioned study on neighborhood violence examined smoking behavior. Results demonstrated that those with high exposure to violence were more likely to report current smoking (odds ratio for those in the medium exposure to violence group: 2.53; high exposure to violence group: 3.08). Similarly, a study conducted with 695 residents (mean age: 39.36) of Central Harlem, New York (Ganz, 2000) found that increased perceptions of neighborhood danger were significantly related to current smoking status. Several other studies have investigated the relation of multiple neighborhood factors of interest and smoking behavior; these are now discussed.

An investigation of 6,814 men and women aged 45-84 (Echeverria, et al., 2008) found that neighborhood problems (a scale that included items of poor physical condition (trash/litter and no sidewalks or poorly maintained sidewalks) and safety (violence)) and social cohesion were significantly related to smoking prevalence. As expected, higher levels of disorder were associated with increased prevalence of this maladaptive health behavior and high levels of social cohesion with lower prevalence. A European study of 5,784 individuals (Miles, 2006) reported that poor physical conditions (labeled as neighborhood disorder) and less perceived safety were related to increased daily smoking, and these effects were more pronounced among men. Finally, social cohesion, neighborhood safety, and the homeplace variable of home safety were associated with smoking behavior among a sample of 793,622 adults (18+ years of age) residing in Minnesota (Patterson, Eberly, Ding, & Hargreaves, 2004). Interestingly, those who responded that they felt unsafe in their home (28.6%) were more likely to smoke than participants who felt unsafe in the neighborhood environment (24.8%), demonstrating the relative importance of homeplace as a safe haven.

Physical Activity

The National Center for Health Statistics classifies leisure-time physical activity into three categories: inactive (*no sessions of light/moderate or vigorous activity of at least 10 minutes duration*), some leisure-time activity (*at least one session of light/moderate or vigorous activity of at least 10 minutes but not meeting the guidelines for regular activity*), and regular leisure-time activity (*3+ sessions per week of vigorous activity lasting at least 20 minutes OR 5+ sessions per week of light/moderate activity of at least 30 minutes duration*) (National Center for Health Statistics, 2009). National data from 2006 demonstrates that although physical activity involvement was higher than previous years, a greater percentage of U.S. adults (18+ years) were inactive (39.5%) than were regularly active (31.0%). As may be expected, physical activity engagement decreased with age and men were more physically active than women.

Ethnic differences in physical activity are apparent, with blacks being more inactive (48.9% vs. 38.2%) and less regularly active (24.9% vs. 31.9%) than whites. However, comparing the 2006 data with that of 2005, whites remained at similar levels while a greater percentage of blacks engaged in physical activity over time. While the ethnic gap remains large, this evidence suggests that it may also be shrinking.

The literature on the relation between physical activity and the neighborhood and homeplace contexts primarily focuses on safety (Cleland, Timperio, & Crawford, 2008; Echeverria, et al., 2008; Eyler, et al., 1998; Eyler, et al., 2003; Foster, Hillsdon, & Thorogood, 2004; Harrison, Gemmell, & Heller, 2007; Hooker, Wilson, Griffin, & Ainsworth, 2005; Humpel, Owen, & Leslie, 2002; King, et al., 2000; Li, Fisher, Brownson, & Bosworth, 2005; Lindstrom Johnson, et al., 2009; McNeill, et al., 2006; Piro, Noess, & Claussen, 2006; Shenassa, Liebhaber, & Ezeamama, 2006; Stark Casagrande, Whitt-Glover, Lancaster, Odoms-Young, & Gary, 2009; Suminski, Carlos Poston, Petosa, Stevens, & Katzenmoyer, 2005; Wilbur, Chandler, Dancy, & Lee, 2003; Wilcox, Bopp, Oberrecht, Kammermann, & McElmurray, 2003) and physical conditions (Addy, et al., 2004; Booth, Owen, Bauman, Clavisi, & Leslie, 2000; Brownson, Baker, Housemann, Brennan, & Bacak, 2001; Cleland, et al., 2008; Echeverria, et al., 2008;

Ellaway, et al., 2005; Humpel, et al., 2002; King, et al., 2000; Li, et al., 2005; McNeill, et al., 2006; Stark Casagrande, et al., 2009; Troped, Saunders, Pate, Reininger, & Addy, 2003). However, empirical work on social cohesion (Addy, et al., 2004; Cleland, et al., 2008; Echeverria, et al., 2008; Poortinga, 2006; Wen, Kandula, & Lauderdale, 2007) and homeplace (Poortinga, 2006) has also been conducted. A brief consideration of a selection of these works follows.

Cleland and colleagues (2008) investigated neighborhood safety, social cohesion, and physical conditions in relation to walking for leisure and transportation. Results demonstrated that perceiving the neighborhood as safe was positively associated with walking for transportation. In terms of leisure walking, physical conditions (in particular, aesthetics) and social cohesion (specifically, trusting local people) demonstrated positive associations. Considering homeplace, Poortinga's (2006) previously discussed study found relations between this context and physical activity. Specifically, in terms of sports activities, homeowners were more likely to be active at least twice a week.

Gender differences in the neighborhood's impact, particularly in relation to issues of safety, on physical activity were identified in several studies (Foster, et al., 2004; Piro, et al., 2006; Shenassa, et al., 2006; Suminski, et al., 2005). In one study, no association between perceived safety and walking was found among men while women were 47% less likely to walk for at least 15 minutes per week if they reported their neighborhood to be unsafe (Foster, et al., 2004). In the remaining studies, significant results were found for both genders; however, differences in these results were evident. Piro and associates (2006) found differences based on the safety measure used as objective neighborhood violence was associated with physical activity only for men and perceived neighborhood safety was related to physical activity only for women. Differences in types of activity by gender were also identified in two studies. One (Shenassa, et al., 2006) found that perceived safety was associated with elevations in the odds of both occasional and frequent exercise among women while it was only related to occasional exercise (not frequent exercise) among men. The second examination (Suminski, et al., 2005) found differences based on walking for exercise versus walking for transportation. Specifically, women's (but not men's) likelihood of walking for exercise was associated with neighborhood safety and men's (but not women's) likelihood of walking for transportation was related to physical conditions of the neighborhood (though this relationship between neighborhood and walking for transportation among men was negative).

Based on the review thus far, neighborhood and homeplace characteristics impact both health behaviors and health outcomes and health behaviors also exert an influence on health outcomes. Therefore, an examination of health behaviors as a mediator in the relationship between the neighborhood and homeplace contexts and health is warranted. The present work examines such a model (Figures 3 & 4), with a further investigation of age, gender, and ethnic differences. In addition, the theories and conceptual models that serve as the basis for this paper (Glass & Balfour, 2003; Lawton, 1982; Lawton & Nahemow, 1973, see also Figures 1 & 2) suggest that personal competences also play an important role in the above relationships. In line with this, the current consideration of environmental impacts on health among adults examines the competency construct of self-efficacy.

Personal Competencies: The Case of Self-Efficacy

While various personal competencies may play a role in the relationship between the environment and health outcomes, self-efficacy is of particular interest as it has become a key component of most theories of health behavior and has been empirically identified as a particularly strong predictor of such behaviors (see for example, Arras, Ogletree, & Welshimer, 2006; Bandura, 1997, 2000; Conner & Norman, 1996; Garcia & Mann, 2003; Schwarzer & Fuchs, 1996). A more detailed examination of the construct of self-efficacy as well as the theory and empirical work that unites self-efficacy and health behaviors follows.

Definition and Theory of Self-Efficacy

The term self-efficacy was first coined by Albert Bandura, who defined the concept as people's beliefs about their ability to perform specific behaviors and exercise control over events (Bandura, 1977, 1989, 1990, 1997, 2000). Self-efficacy is a major determinant of behavior as individuals tend to set goals and perform actions that they consider to be congruent with their capabilities (Bandura, 1977, 1986, 1997, 2000; Conner & Norman, 1996; Maddux, 1995). Furthermore, the effort that one exerts for a particular goal or outcome and the level of one's perseverance in the face of difficulties are impacted by self-efficacy (Bandura, 1977, 1986, 1997; Maddux, 1995; Schwarzer & Fuchs, 1996). Those with a higher level of self-efficacy in a specific domain are more likely to expend effort and persist when setbacks or obstacles arise within that domain.

Self-efficacy is not an inherent trait; rather, it develops as a result of six main sources of influence: mastery experiences, vicarious experiences, imaginal experiences, social persuasion, physiological arousal, and emotional states (Bandura, 1977, 1986, 2000; Maddux, 1995). Mastery experiences (i.e., success at a behavior) are the most effective builder of self-efficacy whereas repeated failures lower beliefs of one's efficacy for the attempted task. Efficacy may also develop as a result of vicarious experiences, through which individuals believe that they can achieve success that is similar to observed social models. The strength of vicarious experiences is impacted by factors such as the perceived similarities between the observer and model, number of models, and power of models. In imaginal experiences, individuals imagine themselves succeeding in a particular domain in future situations. Individuals may be verbally/socially persuaded that they have the abilities to master certain activities. This method of efficacy development is impacted by whether the individual considers the persuader to be an expert, trustworthy, and a reliable source. Aversive physiological arousal is often associated with perceived poor performance, incompetence, and failure while positive physiological states tend to increase confidence and efficacy. Finally, positive affect is likely to enhance efficacy beliefs while negative affect has the opposite effect.

Bandura posits that there are two levels at which self-efficacy influences human health (Bandura, 1997, 2000). At one level, efficacy beliefs (particularly in terms of coping with stressors) activate biological systems that mediate health. Another level is the impact of self-efficacy on the direct control over health behaviors. For the current work, this second level is of primary interest. The present paper also considers potential changes in health-related self-efficacy with aging. Given that individuals experience various physical declines with age, self-efficacy in the health domain may also decrease (however, it is important to note that some declines may be more influenced by self-efficacy than actual biological aging) (Bandura, 1997).

Evidence of the Link between Self-Efficacy and Health Behaviors

Given that self-efficacy theory posits that the construct impacts individuals' actions, effort, and perseverance (Bandura, 1977, 1986, 1997, 2000; Conner & Norman, 1996; Maddux, 1995; Schwarzer & Fuchs, 1996), self-efficacy is expected to influence health behaviors. Indeed, self-efficacy has been found to be a consistent and strong correlate of health behavior (see for example, Arras, et al., 2006; Bandura, 1997; Eyler, et al., 2003; Garcia & Mann, 2003; McNeill, et al., 2006). As the focus of the current paper is on the behaviors of smoking and physical activity, a representative portion of the empirical work on self-efficacy in relation to these variables is considered.

Self-efficacy has shown relations with smoking in terms of intention to quit, abstinence success, and relapse, with those with high self-efficacy demonstrating more adaptive outcomes (see for example, Berg, Sanderson Cox, Mahnken, Greiner, & Ellerbeck, 2008; Boardman, Catley, Mayo, & Ahluwalia, 2005; Gwaltney, Metrik, Kahler, & Shiffman, 2009; Gwaltney, Shiffman, Balabanis, & Paty, 2005; Marlatt & Donovan, 2005; O'Hea, et al., 2004; Ockene, et al., 2000). Given that self-efficacy is a dynamic (rather than fixed) trait, one study (Gwaltney, et al., 2005) examined daily abstinence self-efficacy among 305 smokers (mean age: 39.5) in a smoking cessation clinic. The results confirmed that variations in daily self-efficacy predicted lapse and subsequent relapse, demonstrating the importance of the maintenance of self-efficacy over time.

Physical activity-specific self-efficacy has been related to physical activity as an outcome (see for example, Booth, et al., 2000; Duncan & Mummery, 2005; Eyler, et al., 2003; McNeill, et al., 2006; Morris, McAuley, & Motl, 2008; Wilcox, et al., 2003).

Furthermore, it appears as though the strength of the relationship increases as the level of activity intensity increases (McNeill, et al., 2006). Some evidence also points to self-efficacy as a potential mediator between the environment and physical activity (McNeill, et al., 2006; Morris, et al., 2008). For example, a 6-month observational study of 137 women (mean age: 69.6) found that changes in neighborhood satisfaction (which included perceptions of the pleasantness of the neighborhood) affected changes in self-efficacy, and changes in self-efficacy in turn were associated with increased physical activity over time (Morris, et al., 2008).

As evidenced by this review of the relevant literature, significant relationships have been found among the neighborhood/homeplace, self-efficacy, health behaviors, and health outcomes. However, the interrelations of these variables, as well as the individual differences in these interrelations, have not been fully specified. As previously mentioned, the goals of this work include: 1. To examine the relationships among the neighborhood context and individual characteristics that impact health; 2. To determine whether differences in the person-neighborhood interaction are apparent with aging; 3. To test potential gender, ethnicity, and education differences in health based on the relationship between the context and the individual. In addressing these goals, theoretically- and empirically-based research questions and hypotheses will be investigated.

3. Research Questions & Hypotheses

Based on the reviewed theories and research findings, the following research questions and hypotheses have been posed:

Research Question 1: What role does health behaviors play in the relationship between neighborhood/homeplace and health?

Hypothesis 1 (H1): Neighborhood/homeplace effects on health will be mediated by health behaviors.

Research Question 2: Does health-related self-efficacy mediate the relationship between neighborhood/homeplace and health behaviors?

Hypothesis 2 (H2): Health-related self-efficacy will serve as a mediator in the association between neighborhood/homeplace and health behaviors.

Research Question 3 (alternate model): Does health-related self-efficacy moderate the relationship between neighborhood/homeplace and health behaviors?

Hypothesis 3a (H3a): Among individuals with low health-related self-efficacy, poor neighborhood conditions will have a maladaptive impact on health behaviors and, hence, health outcomes.

Hypothesis 3b (H3b): This moderation effect will be stronger in magnitude with increasing age.

Research Question 4: Do gender, education, and race/ethnicity differences exist in the model?

For these demographic differences, no hypotheses are posited. Therefore, this examination will be exploratory in nature.

4. Methods

The National Survey of Midlife Development in the United States (MIDUS)

The National Survey of Midlife Development in the United States (MIDUS), carried out by the MacArthur Midlife Research Network, was designed to investigate behavioral, psychological, and social influences on midlife development, health, and well-being. The first wave of the study (MIDUS I) was collected from 1994 to 1996. This wave included a general sample, siblings of those in the general sample, a twin sample, and an additional minority sample. Given that several of the measures of interest were not collected in the additional minority sample, participants from that sample are not included in the current paper. Here, I define the MIDUS I "primary sample" as the general sample, siblings, and twins.

Participants

The MIDUS I primary sample is composed of 7,108 non-institutionalized English-speaking adults aged 20-75 (Mean: 46.38; SD: 13). The life stage periods of young adulthood (<35 yrs; n= 1,526 (21.6%)), early midlife (35-50 yrs; n= 2,922 (41.5%)), late midlife (51-65 yrs; n= 1,910 (27.1%)), and late life (>65 yrs; n= 691 (9.8%)) are represented, with a majority of the sample being middle aged. The gender split is nearly equal with 3,395 (47.8%) male and 3,632 (51.1%) female respondents (81 participants (1.1%) did not indicate their gender). Of the 6,176 participants who provided their ethnicity, 5,600 (78.8%) are White, 321 (4.5%) Black, 37 (.5%) Native American, 57 (.8%) Asian/Pacific Islander, 42 (.6%) Multiracial, and 119 (1.7%) responded Other. The education level of the respondents was as follows: 9.6% did not graduate high school, 28.9% graduated from high school (1.5% of these obtained a GED), 23%

attended college but did not obtain a degree, 7.6% received an associate's degree, 17.4% obtained a bachelor's degree, and 13.3% attended graduate/professional school (data was missing for 0.2%).

Data Collection

The method of random-digit-dialing was applied to the working telephone banks in the coterminous United States in order to recruit participants for the general sample. One individual was interviewed per household. The random respondent was interviewed or rejected based on the ease of obtaining individuals of similar gender and age. For example, all males between 65 and 74 years of age were interviewed given that this subsample was rare. On the other hand, half of the females aged 25-34 were rejected due to the large number of respondents in this category. Of the participants with siblings, 529 were randomly selected to provide contact information for their sibling(s), leading to 951 siblings (with the same biological parents) identified. The general participants were asked to contact their sibling(s) about the study prior to the recruiter's telephone call in order to aid in recruitment. To recruit twins, 50,000 households were screened to identify twins within the family. Recruiters then contacted a member of the twin pair; those who cooperated were asked to provide contact information for their twin.

All participants conducted a telephone interview that was, on average, 30 minutes in length. Then, self-administered questionnaires (with an estimated average time commitment of 2 hours) were mailed to the participants along with a pen and check for $20. A reminder postcard, copy of the questionnaire with a letter requesting its return, and a reminder telephone call were used to increase response. In the final reminder telephone call, individuals (one-fourth of cases) were offered an additional $100 to complete the interview. The response rate for the telephone interview was 70%. Of these telephone respondents, 86.8% completed the questionnaire, leading to an overall response rate of 60.8%.

Sample & Measures of the Current Study

Participants

The demographic characteristics of the study sample are presented in Table 1. The focus of the current study is on health among blacks and whites and, therefore, participants of other ethnic groups were not included. The study sample includes 5,600 whites and 321 blacks. Similar to the primary sample, the age range of the study sample is 20-75, with a slightly higher mean of 47.14. In terms of life stage periods, the sample is categorized as follows: 19.5% (n= 1,152) in young adulthood (<35 yrs.), 41.7% (n= 2,472) in early midlife (35-50 yrs.), 28.3% (n= 1,675) in late midlife (51-65 yrs), and 10.5% (n= 621) in late life (>65 yrs). The gender split of the sample is 47.4% (n=2,804) male and 52.6% (n= 3,117) female. For the study sample, the education level was as follows: 8.6% did not graduate high school, 29.0% graduated from high school (1.3% of these obtained a GED), 22.6% attended college but did not obtain a degree, 7.7% received an associate's degree, 18.3% obtained a bachelor's degree, and 13.8% attended graduate/professional school (data was missing for 0.2%).

Table 1. Demographic Characteristics of the Study Participants (N= 5921)

Age (yrs.), *mean*	47.14
Race *n (%)*	
White	5600 (94.6%)
Black	321 (5.4%)
Gender *n (%)*	
Male	2804 (47.4%)
Female	3117 (52.6%)
Education[a] *n (%)*	
No school/some grade school	22 (.4%)
Eighth grade/junior high school	90 (1.5%)
Some high school	396 (6.7%)
GED	77 (1.3%)
Graduated from high school	1638 (27.7%)
1 to 2 years of college, no degree	1069 (18.1%)
3 or more years of college, no degree	268 (4.5%)
Graduated 2 year college/vocational school or associates degree	455 (7.7%)
Graduated 4 or 5 year college or bachelors degree	1083 (18.3%)
Some graduate school	165 (2.8%)
Masters degree	431 (7.3%)
Professional degree	217 (3.7%)

Note: [a] Education data were missing for 10 participants

Measures

    Neighborhood & Homeplace Factors. Neighborhood safety and social cohesion items were taken from Keyes' (1998) paper on social well-being. Physical conditions items with a matching format were added to this measure for the MIDUS study. All of the items were rated on a scale from 1 ("A lot") to 4 ("Not at all"); however, the responses were anchored at 0, resulting in a range from 0 ("A lot") to 3 ("Not at all"). *Safety* was assessed through the rating of the following statements: "I feel safe being out alone in my neighborhood during the daytime" and "I feel safe being out alone in my neighborhood at night". For the current analyses, these two items were reverse-coded and combined, resulting in a range from 0-6 (higher values reflecting greater perceived safety). The two *Physical conditions* statements were "Buildings and streets in my neighborhood are kept in very good repair" and "My neighborhood is kept clean". The items were reverse-coded and a composite (range 0-6) was made, with higher values indicating better physical conditions. To measure neighborhood-level *Social cohesion*, participants responded to the statements "I could call on a neighbor for help if I needed it" and "People in my neighborhood trust each other". These two items were reverse-coded and combined, resulting in a range of 0-6, with higher values representing greater social cohesion. *Homeplace* questions included "I live in as nice a home as most people", "I'm proud of my home", "I don't like to invite people to my home because I do not live in a very nice place", and "I feel very good about my home and neighborhood". These items were reverse-coded (except for the third item) and a composite score was taken, resulting in a range from 0-12 (with higher scores indicating more positive perceptions of homeplace). Given that homeownership is an indicator of attachment to place (Burton & Lawson Clark, 2005), participants were also asked whether they owned their home outright, were paying on a mortgage, or rented. For the current work, renting was scored as 0, paying on a mortgage was scored as 1, and owning a home was scored as 2.

Self-efficacy. In the present work, six items from the questionnaire are utilized to determine health-specific *Self-efficacy*. Using a 7-point scale, ranging from 1 ("Strongly agree") to 7 ("Strongly disagree"), participants rated their agreement to the following statements: 1. "Keeping healthy depends on things that I can do", 2. "There are certain things I can do for myself to reduce the risk of a heart attack", 3. "There are certain things I can do for myself to reduce the risk of getting cancer", 4. "I work hard at trying to stay healthy", 5. "When I am sick, getting better is in the doctor's hands", and 6. "It is difficult for me to get good medical care". These items were anchored at zero. In addition, the items were reverse-coded (except for items 5 and 6) so that higher scores represented greater health-specific self-efficacy.

Health Behaviors. Three questions were utilized to assess *Smoking* behavior. Participants were first asked "At what age did you have your very first cigarette?" Individuals who responded that they never had a cigarette were classified as "never smoked". Then, to distinguish ex-smokers from current smokers, individuals were asked two questions. The first question was "Have you ever smoked cigarettes regularly- that is, at least a few cigarettes every day?" The second question was "Do you smoke cigarettes regularly now?" Both of these questions were answered using the yes/no format. For the current paper, individuals who responded "yes" to the first question and "no" to the second question were labeled "ex-smokers" and participants who responded "yes" to the second question were categorized as "current smokers". *Physical activity*, a health-promoting behavior, was measured with four items that assessed vigorous (e.g., running, lifting heavy objects) and moderate (e.g., bowling, using a vacuum cleaner) physical activity during the summer and winter seasons. The response set for these four questions was (1) "Several times a week or more", (2) "About once a week", (3) "Several times a week", (4) "About once a month", (5) "Less than once a month", and (6) "Never". For the current paper, these values were anchored at zero and reverse-coded. The two vigorous activity items were combined (resulting in a scale from 0-10, with higher scores indicating more physical activity) and the two moderate activity items were combined (resulting in a scale from 0-10, with higher scores indicating more physical activity).

Health. Self-rated health was assessed with one question, "Using a scale from 0 to 10 where 0 means 'the worst possible health' and 10 means 'the best possible health', how would you rate your health these days?" For the current work, the item was reverse-coded so that higher values indicated worse self-rated health. A list of chronic conditions was provided in the questionnaire and participants were asked to indicate (yes/no response) whether they had experienced or been treated for each of the conditions in the past year. From this list, "High blood pressure or hypertension" was chosen as one of the three indicators of *Cardiovascular disease* for the present study. Two other indicators were measured with the yes/no response questions "Have you ever had heart trouble suspected or confirmed by a doctor?" and "Have you ever had a heart attack?" For the current analysis, a response of "no" was coded as 0 while a response of "yes" was coded as 1. The numbers were then summed, resulting in a 0-3 scale, with higher values denoting worse cardiovascular health. In addition, waist size, a common indicator of cardiovascular disease (see, for example, de Koning, Merchant, Pogue, & Anand, 2007; Nelson, Brandon, Wiggins, & Whitfield, 2002), was recorded in inches and rounded to the nearest whole number. To measure *Obesity*, using the participants' responses to height and weight, BMI was calculated as weight in kilograms divided by height in meters squared. Those with a BMI greater than or equal to 30 kilograms/meter^2 are classified as obese.

5. Statistical Analysis

Descriptive Statistics

Descriptive statistics were conducted to examine the mean, standard deviation, and distribution of the variables of interest (neighborhood/homeplace variables: safety, physical conditions, social cohesion, homeplace, and homeownership; health-related self-efficacy; health behavior variables: smoking, vigorous physical activity, and moderate physical activity; health outcome variables: self-rated health, obesity, cardiovascular disease, and waist size). Then, a correlation matrix was produced to examine the correlations among these variables as well as the demographic variables. These analyses were conducted with SPSS version 19.

Structural Equation Modeling

Structural equation modeling (SEM) has a number of strengths as an analytic tool (see Hoyle, 1995; Tomarken & Waller, 2005). First, it is appropriate for complex models that would require multiple smaller tests with other methods (e.g., multiple regression). Second, it allows for the testing of relationships among observed and latent factors. Third, SEM corrects for random and measurement error. Given these characteristics of SEM, this analytic technique was used to test the hypothesized models. SEM was conducted using Mplus version 4.1.

Estimation

For the analyses of the current dissertation, the Maximum Likelihood (ML) estimator was employed. This estimation method is the most commonly used and has been recommended by Hoyle and Panter (1995). This estimator assumes that the distribution of the observed variables is multivariate normal, and in such cases is unbiased, consistent, and efficient (Anderson & Gerbing, 1988; Kline, 2005). Using this estimation method, various parameter values are considered and those that maximize the likelihood of the observed data are selected (Ferron & Hess, 2007; Kline, 2005).

Evaluation of Model Fit

Several fit indices were utilized to assess model fit. Based on Hoyle and Panter's (1995) recommendations, an absolute index and two incremental indices are reported. Absolute indices demonstrate the degree to which the implied covariances of the model match the observed covariances of the data (Hoyle & Panter, 1995). The recommended absolute index is the χ^2 goodness-of-fit test (Bollen, 1989; Satorra & Bentler, 1994). With the χ^2, the degrees of freedom, sample size, and p-value are also reported. For this index, the optimal χ^2 value is zero; therefore, increasing χ^2 values indicate less optimal fit (Hoyle & Panter, 1995). In addition, p-values <.05 demonstrate that the specified model does not fit the data; therefore, non-significant p-values indicate better fit. Incremental indices demonstrate the degree to which the specified model is superior to the null model (i.e., no covariances among variables) in terms of reproducing the observed data (Hoyle & Panter, 1995). The incremental indices that were interpreted include the Comparative Fit Index (CFI) (Bentler, 1989, 1990) and the Tucker-Lewis Index (TLI) (Tucker & Lewis, 1973). For both of these indices, a value of .90 or higher indicates model fit. In addition to these recommended indices, the Root Mean Square Error of Approximation (RMSEA) (Steiger, 1990; Steiger & Lind, 1980) was examined. This fit index represents the fit per degree of freedom of the model. In terms of RMSEA, a value ≤.05 indicates good model fit and a value between .05 and .08 indicates acceptable fit, whereas models with an RMSEA of 1.0 or greater have poor fit (Browne & Cudeck, 1990). Of note, the

χ^2 test is sensitive to sample size and may be significant due to the large size of the sample (Hu & Bentler, 1995; Kline, 2005). Therefore, the CFI, TLI, and RMSEA fit indices were primarily utilized to determine fit.

SEM Analysis Step 1: The Measurement Model

The confirmatory measurement model specifies the posited relations of the observed variables and the latent variables. To examine these relations, a confirmatory factor analysis was conducted. For a depiction of the proposed relations between observed variables and latent constructs, see Figure 5.

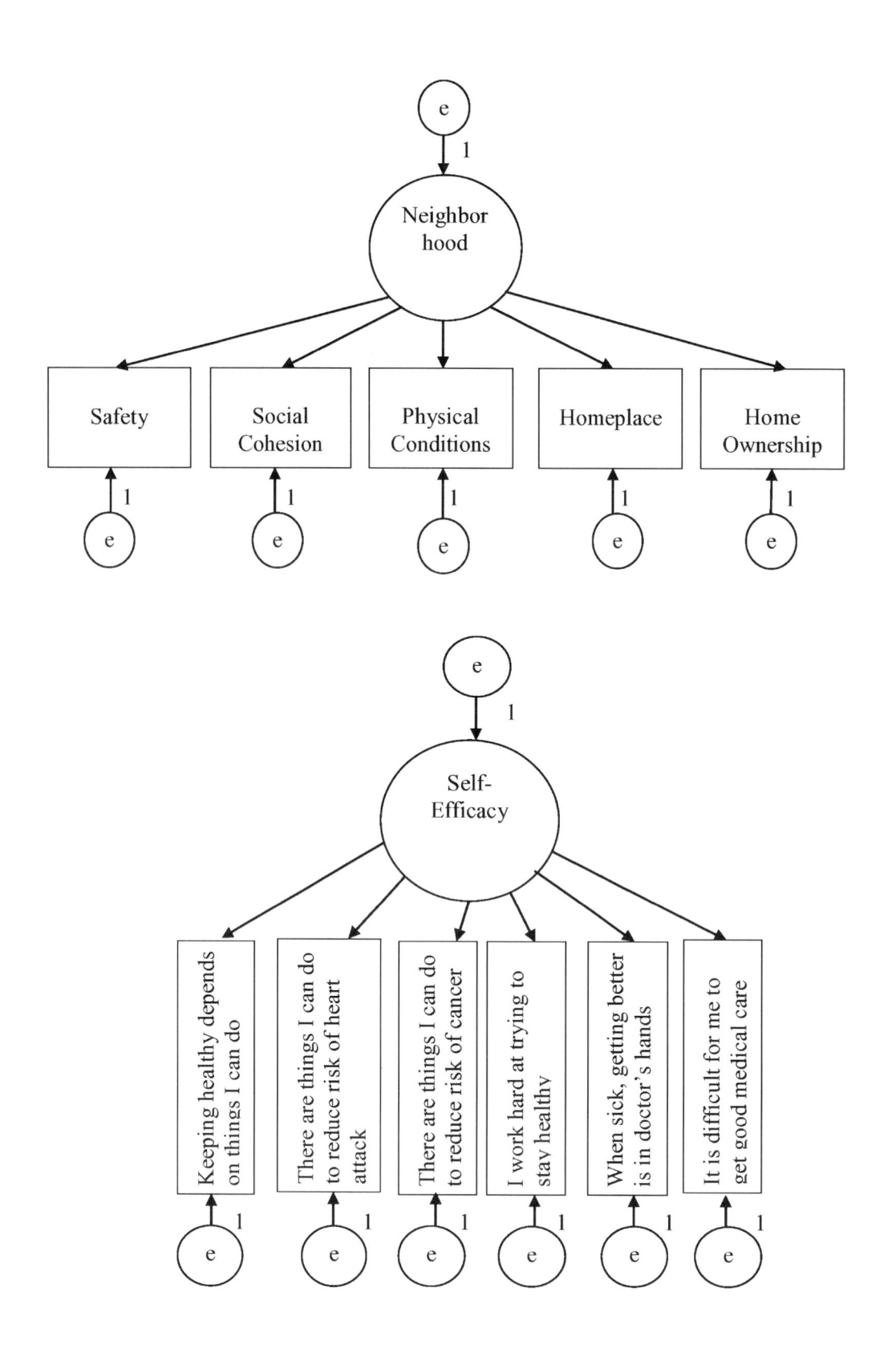

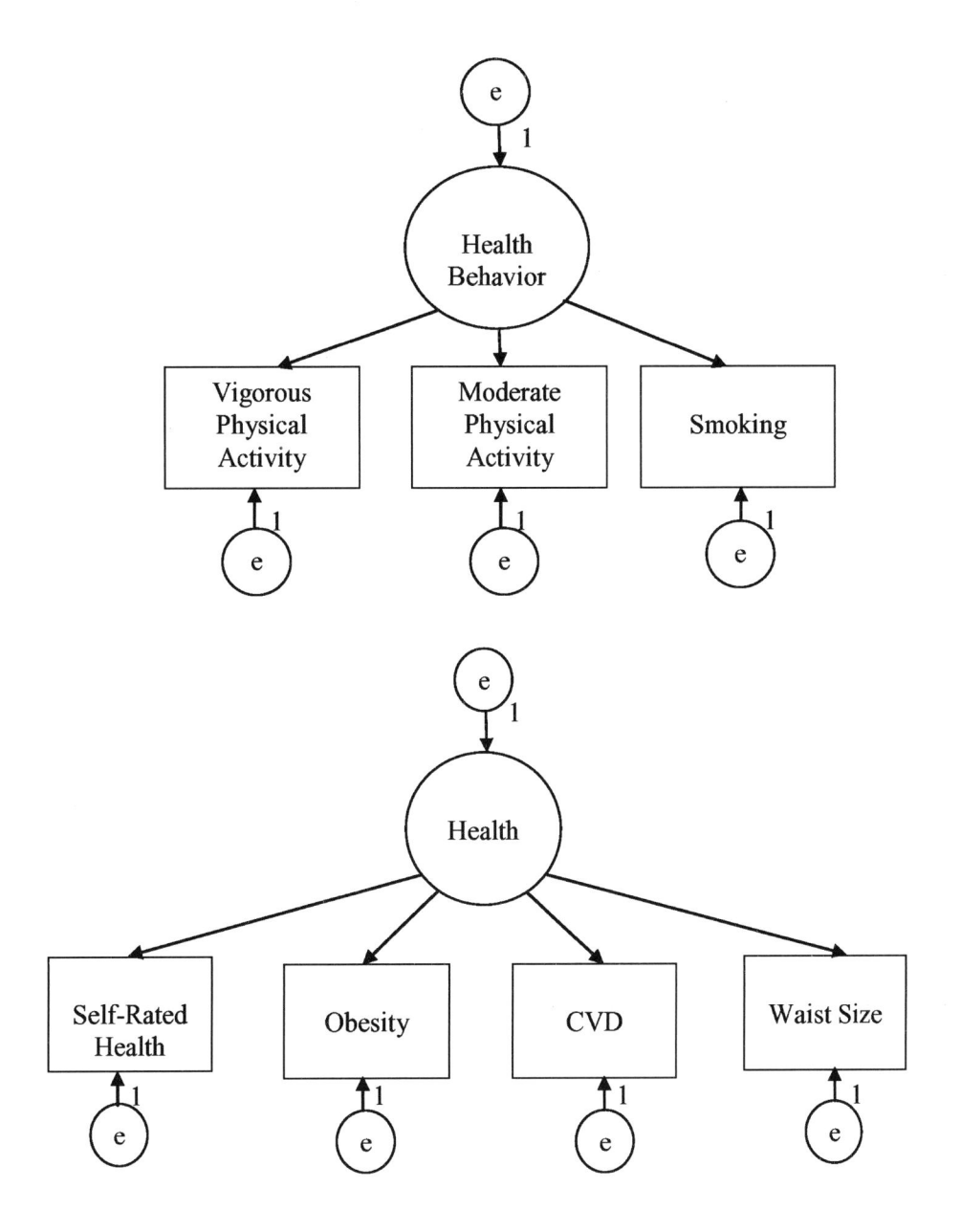

Figure 5. The Measurement Model

SEM Analysis Step 2: Structural Model 1

In the next step, structural model 1 (see Figure 3) was tested. This examined whether health behaviors mediate the relationship between neighborhood/homeplace and health (H1) and whether health-related self-efficacy mediates the relationship between neighborhood/homeplace and health behaviors (H2a).

SEM Analysis Step 3: Structural Model 2

Following the test of the first structural model, the alternate structural model (model 2; see Figure 4) was tested to determine which of the two models best fit the observed data. This second test examined whether health behaviors mediate the relationship between neighborhood/homeplace and health (H1) and whether health-related self-efficacy moderates the relationship between neighborhood/homeplace and health behaviors (H3). For this test, a latent class analysis was conducted to categorize participants as high in self-efficacy or low in self-efficacy.

SEM Analysis Step 4: Testing Demographic Differences

Demographic differences in terms of age, gender, ethnicity, and education were tested in the model that exhibited the best fit with the data, addressing research question 4. To perform these tests, the model was separately tested for each group (i.e., for the age test: young adulthood, early midlife, late midlife, and older adulthood; for the gender test: males and females; for the ethnicity test: whites and blacks; for the education test: did not graduate high school, graduated high school, some college, and graduate college and above) and then compared.

6. Results

Descriptive Statistics

The means and standard deviations of the study variables are displayed at the bottom of Table 2. An examination of the descriptive statistics for the neighborhood variables demonstrates that the participants' perceptions of their neighborhood environment were generally positive. This is particularly evident for neighborhood safety as the mean was 5.17 (with a standard deviation of 1.16) on a 6-point scale. Neighborhood physical conditions and social cohesion showed slightly more variability but were also rated quite high on the scale (M=4.93, SD=1.29 and M=4.58, SD=1.42, respectively). The homeownership variable shows that more participants paid on a mortgage than rented or owned a home. The frequencies of this indicator support this interpretation as approximately 53% of the participants paid on a mortgage, 21% rented, and 24% owned a home (data were missing for roughly 2% of the sample). The ratings of homeplace also demonstrate positive perceptions. On a 12-point scale, the mean was 10.21 (with a standard deviation of 2.27). These statistics indicate that, in general, participants considered their neighborhoods to be safe, in good physical condition, and socially cohesive and experienced a strong sense of homeplace.

Six items were used to measure health-related self-efficacy (all of these items were scored from 0=strongly disagree to 6=strongly agree). Participants largely agreed that health depends on things they can do and that they can do things that reduce the risk of heart attack (M=5.41, SD= .97 and M=5.63, SD=.85, respectively). Lower mean levels of efficacy and greater variability were found for the items related to reducing the risk of cancer (M=4.90, SD=1.30), working hard to stay healthy (M=4.60, SD=1.32), and obtaining good medical care (M=4.22, SD=2.01). Of the items, participants experienced the lowest levels of efficacy in terms of the statement "When I am sick, getting better is in the doctor's hands" (M=3.19, SD=1.96).

Table 2. Descriptive Statistics, Correlations with Demographic Variables, and Correlations with Other Indicators of Latent Variables for 18 Indicators of Latent Variables

	1	2	3	4	5	6	7	8	9	10	11	12	13	14	15	16	17	18	19	20
1.Age	1																			
2.Edu	-.11	1																		
3.NS	-.01	.13	1																	
4.NPC	.14	.10	.36	1																
5.NSC	.23	.01	.33	.42	1															
6.HO	.44	-.04	.12	.14	.30	1														
7.HP	.17	.04	.36	.60	.48	.25	1													
8.SE1	-.06	.06	.10	.09	.07	-.01	.09	1												
9.SE2	-.09	.09	.11	.08	.06	-.02	.08	.61	1											
10.SE3	-.05	.08	.08	.07	.07	-.01	.05	.41	.50	1										
11.SE4	.16	.01	.04	.14	.16	.10	.18	.31	.30	.27	1									
12.SE5	-.24	.15	.03*	-.05	-.09	-.13	-.06	-.04	-.02	-.02	-.18	1								
13.SE6	-.01	.13	.12	.16	.14	.05	.16	.08	.08	.04	.02	.08	1							
14.VPA	-.27	.17	.17	.03*	.04	-.06	.06	.13	.09	.10	.18	.10	.05	1						
15.MPA	-.20	.17	.13	.07	.06	-.01	.07	.12	.12	.10	.14	.10	.08	.49	1					
16.SS	.03	.25	.00	.08	.08	.11	.08	.05	.05	.01	.19	.01	.11	.05	.08	1				
17.SRH	.03*	-.09	-.15	-.16	-.16	-.06	-.20	-.15	-.11	-.12	-.25	-.02	-.15	-.26	-.25	-.14	1			
18.CVD	.30	-.10	-.05	-.02	.03*	.11	-.01	-.04	-.05	-.07	.02	-.13	-.02	-.18	-.16	-.00	.27	1		
19.BMI	.10	-.11	-.03*	-.07	-.06	.02	-.06	-.05	-.02	-.06	-.20	-.04	-.03*	-.15	-.15	.07	.24	.18	1	
20.WS	.20	-.07	.05	-.05	-.04	.07	-.04	-.06	-.04	-.07	-.21	-.05	-.03	-.12	-.19	.01	.24	.21	.80	1
M	47.14	6.86	5.17	4.93	4.58	1.04	10.21	5.41	5.63	4.90	4.60	3.19	4.22	6.30	8.50	1.03	2.53	.31	26.65	35.43
SD	12.92	2.47	1.16	1.29	1.42	.68	2.27	.97	.85	1.30	1.32	1.96	2.01	3.44	2.19	.78	1.61	.58	5.26	5.74

Bold correlations are significant at the 0.01 level; * Correlation is significant at the 0.05 level.
Edu= Education; NS= Neighborhood Safety; NPC= Neighborhood Physical Conditions; NSC= Neighborhood Social Cohesion; HO= Homeownership; HP= Homeplace; SE1= Self-efficacy 1: Keeping healthy depends on things that I can do; SE2= Self-efficacy 2: There are certain things I can do for myself to reduce the risk of a heart attack; SE3= Self-efficacy 3: There are certain things I can do for myself to reduce the risk of getting cancer; SE4= Self-efficacy 4: I work hard at trying to stay healthy; SE5= Self-efficacy 5: When I am sick, getting better is in the doctor's hands; SE6= Self-efficacy 6: It is difficult for me to get good medical care; VPA= Vigorous Physical Activity; MPA= Moderate Physical Activity; SS= Smoking Status; SRH= Self-rated Health; CVD= Cardiovascular Disease; BMI= Body Mass Index; WS= Waist Size; M= Mean; SD= Standard Deviation.

Examining the health behavior of physical activity, participation in moderate physical activity was quite high, with a mean of 8.50 and a standard deviation of 2.19 on a 0-10 scale (0=never, 10=several times a week or more). As would be expected, compared to moderate activity, vigorous physical activity participation was lower and more variable (M=6.30, SD=3.44, using the same scale). Given that only 1.9% of the sample stated that they never participated in moderate physical activity, the activity level of the sample is higher than the general population (based on data from 2006 that 39.5% of the population 18+ yrs. was inactive (National Center for Health Statistics, 2009); however, it must be noted that the definitions vary by measure). Examining the maladaptive health behavior of smoking, the mean was 1.03 with a standard deviation of .78. This suggests that each of the smoking groups was nearly equally represented, as is supported by the frequencies: 23.8% never smoked, 29.9% previously smoked, and 21.4% currently smoked (data were missing for 24.9% of the sample).

The health outcomes of interest include self-rated health, cardiovascular disease, and obesity. The descriptive statistics of the items associated with these outcomes demonstrate that the sample was relatively healthy. Self-rated health was scored on a 0-10 scale that ranged from 0=best health to 10=worst health. The mean of this item was 2.53, with a standard deviation of 1.61, indicating that participants generally considered themselves to be in good health. For the count of cardiovascular conditions, a majority of individuals did not suffer from cardiovascular disease. This is evident by the percentage of individuals who had zero cardiovascular diseases (73.2%) compared to those who had one (19.9%), two (4.0%), or three (.7%) indicators of heart problems (data were missing for 2.2% of the sample). The mean waist size of the sample was 35.43 (SD= 5.74). In terms of body mass index, the mean was 26.65 with a standard deviation of 5.26. Underweight is defined as a BMI <18.5, normal weight as 18.5-25, overweight as >25, and obesity as ≥ 30. For the current sample, approximately 2% were underweight, 43% were normal weight, 29% were overweight (not including obesity), and 22% were obese (resulting in 51% overweight including obesity) (data were missing for roughly 4% of the sample). These values indicate that the sample was of healthier weight than the general population, as evident by the most recently available U.S. population statistics from 2003-2006: 31.6% normal weight, 33.4% obese, and 66.7% overweight including obesity (it should be noted that these data are for individuals 20+ yrs.) (National Center for Health Statistics, 2009).

Correlations

All correlations are presented in Table 2. To ease the presentation of the correlation findings, they will be discussed separately for correlations with demographic variables, correlations of indicators within latent constructs, and correlations across indicators of latent constructs.

Indicator Correlations with Demographic Variables

The demographic variables that were included in the correlation matrix include age and education level. The age correlations demonstrate that an increase in age was associated with an increase in positive perceptions about the neighborhood and homeplace, except for neighborhood safety, which was not significantly correlated with age. Examining the self-efficacy variables, age was not correlated with difficulty in obtaining good medical care. Unexpectedly, age was positively correlated with the self-efficacy measure of working hard to stay healthy. This finding may suggest that individuals must work harder to remain healthy as they age due to the natural (or disease-related) physical declines that occur with aging. However, as expected, age was negatively correlated with the remaining self-efficacy items. Age was not correlated with the health behavior of smoking; however, a significant negative correlation was found for both vigorous and moderate physical activity. For all of the health outcomes, an increase in age was associated with worse health.

For most of the correlations with education, findings were in the expected direction. Although education was not correlated with neighborhood social cohesion, it was positively correlated with perceived neighborhood safety, physical conditions, and homeplace. An unexpected finding was that as education level increased, homeownership decreased. However, in the current sample, the high positive correlation between age and homeownership and the negative correlation between age and education may explain this result. For self-efficacy, education was not correlated with working hard to stay healthy. However, higher levels of education were associated with greater self-efficacy for the remaining five items. Higher education level was also associated with more adaptive health behaviors (for both indicators of physical activity and smoking) and better health outcomes.

Correlations of Indicators within Latent Constructs

The latent constructs of the current work include neighborhood/homeplace, health-related self-efficacy, health behaviors, and health. Correlations among indicators within each of these latent variables may suggest a greater likelihood that these indicators measure the posited latent constructs (which will later be tested using confirmatory factor analysis). Within the neighborhood/homeplace construct, all of the indicators were positively correlated with each other.

Among the self-efficacy measures, three correlations were not significant: 1. reducing the risk of heart attack and getting better is in the doctor's hands; 2. reducing the risk of cancer and getting better is in the doctor's hands; 3. working hard to stay healthy and obtaining good medical care. Furthermore, beliefs about whether getting better is in the doctor's hands demonstrated a negative correlation with the perception that one can do things to keep healthy and working hard to stay healthy. However, the remaining relationships among the self-efficacy variables were positive. Given the non-significant and unexpected negative findings for the item "When sick, getting better is in the doctor's hands", this item may not be a good indicator of health-related self-efficacy in the measurement model.

An examination of the health behaviors shows that all of the indicators were positively correlated. Although the correlations between the physical activity measures and smoking status were quite low, moderate physical activity and vigorous physical activity demonstrated a moderate correlation. For the health outcome indicators of self-rated health, cardiovascular disease, body mass index, and waist size, all of these variables were positively correlated with each other. Furthermore, a high correlation was demonstrated between body mass index and waist size. This result is not surprising given that waist size is a measure of abdominal obesity and body mass index measures general obesity.

Correlations across Indicators of Latent Constructs

First, the correlations of all neighborhood/homeplace, self-efficacy, and health behavior indicators with the health outcome variables are discussed. Then, the correlations among the neighborhood/homeplace variables and the self-efficacy and health behavior variables are presented. Finally, the correlations between the self-efficacy and health behavior indicators are provided.

Neighborhood safety was associated with better health for all indicators except waist size, for which greater safety was associated with larger waist size. The correlations between neighborhood physical conditions and the health indicators were all significant (with better conditions related to better health), except for cardiovascular disease (which was non-significant). Cardiovascular disease also evidenced an unexpected association with neighborhood social cohesion such that greater cohesion was related to greater cardiovascular disease. However, all other health correlations with social cohesion were in the expected direction. For the homeplace indicators, two correlations were not significant: 1. perceived homeplace and cardiovascular disease and 2. homeownership and body mass index. The remaining correlations with perceived homeplace demonstrated that an increased sense of homeplace was associated with better health. Interestingly, however, only self-rated health showed the expected relation with homeownership as increased homeownership was related to worse health in terms of cardiovascular disease and waist size.

The correlations between self-efficacy and health outcomes indicate that all of the significant findings were in the expected direction, with greater self-efficacy associated with better health outcomes. However, some of the correlations did not reach significance (beliefs about reducing the risk of heart attack and BMI; working hard to stay healthy and cardiovascular disease; beliefs about whether getting better is in the doctor's hands and self-rated health; difficulty with obtaining good medical care and cardiovascular disease and waist size).

Both moderate and vigorous physical activity were associated with all of the health outcome indicators, with greater physical activity related to better health. Smoking status demonstrated more variable findings. Smoking status was not correlated with cardiovascular disease or waist size. While smoking showed the expected relationship with self-rated health (increased smoking was associated with worse health), less smoking behavior was associated with an increase in BMI. While this might seem counterintuitive at first, cigarette smoking has been associated with weight maintenance as smoking cessation often results in weight gain (Flegal, Troiano, Pamuk, Kuczmarski, & Campbell, 1995; Wane, van Uffelen, & Brown, 2010; Williamson, et al., 1991), which may explain this finding.

Now that the relationships among the health outcome variables and all other indicators have been presented, an examination of the correlations between neighborhood/homeplace and self-efficacy and health behaviors is undertaken. For the most part, correlations were in the expected direction, with better neighborhood/homeplace perceptions associated with higher levels of self-efficacy. However, a few of the variables did not evidence this relationship. Homeownership was not correlated with beliefs about keeping healthy depends on things one can do, reducing the risk of heart attack, or reducing the risk of cancer. Furthermore, higher rated neighborhood physical conditions, social cohesion, homeownership, and perceived homeplace were associated with greater beliefs that getting better is in the doctor's hands.

When considering the correlations between neighborhood/homeplace and health behaviors, higher scores on the context variables were related to more adaptive health behaviors. Exceptions include two non-significant correlations (neighborhood safety and smoking status; homeownership and moderate physical activity) and one correlation that was in the unexpected direction (homeownership was related to less vigorous physical activity).

Finally, the self-efficacy variables demonstrated the expected relationships with the health behavior variables. Greater levels of health-related self-efficacy were related to more adaptive health behaviors for all relationships except for two (beliefs about reducing the risk of cancer and smoking status; beliefs about whether getting better is in the doctor's hands and smoking status), which were non-significant. Overall, generally speaking, the indicators within latent constructs are correlated and most of the correlations across latent variables are positive and in the expected direction. These correlation results provide some support for the hypothesized models, which will be further investigated using structural equation modeling.

Structural Equation Modeling Results

Confirmatory Factor Analysis

The confirmatory factor analysis resulted in modifications to each of the proposed latent constructs. In the first analysis, the model fit was poor according to the fit statistics: N= 5921; χ^2= 3877.52, df= 129, p<.001; CFI= .839; TLI= .809; RMSEA= .070. A standardized loading of .40 demonstrates that an indicator loads onto a latent construct. For the neighborhood latent factor, the homeownership indicator did not significantly load onto the factor (standardized loading: .298) and was, therefore, dropped. For the self-efficacy latent factor, two items did not have significant loadings: "When I am sick, getting better is in the doctor's hands" (-.047) and "It is difficult for me to get good medical care" (.104). The smoking status item did not significantly load onto the health behavior latent construct (.096); therefore, only physical activity indicators remained in this factor and the latent variable was relabeled as physical activity. The latent construct of health was not confirmed and, therefore, the indicators were examined as individual observed outcome variables in the structural models. Finally, modification indices suggested that the errors of vigorous physical activity and neighborhood safety should be allowed to covary.

Based on these initial results, four indicators (safety, social cohesion, physical conditions, and homeplace) were retained in the neighborhood latent construct; four variables ("Keeping healthy depends on things that I can do", "There are certain things I can do for myself to reduce the risk of a heart attack", "There are certain things I can do for myself to reduce the risk of getting cancer", and "I work hard at trying to stay healthy") remained in the self-efficacy latent variable; and two indicators (vigorous physical activity and moderate physical activity) informed the latent construct of physical activity. The resulting measurement model achieved model fit (N= 5921; χ^2= 510.90, df= 31, p<.001; CFI= .964; TLI= .947; RMSEA= .051). Then, using this measurement model, the structural models were estimated.

Structural Model 1

The first structural model posited that 1. self-efficacy mediates the relationships between neighborhood and physical activity and 2. physical activity mediates the association between neighborhood and the health outcomes of self-rated health, body mass index, waist size, and cardiovascular disease. The structural equation modeling findings indicated that this model fit the data (N= 5921; χ^2= 1159.63, df= 63, p<.001; CFI= .948; TLI= .926; RMSEA= .054). Both the CFI and TLI were above the .90 value, indicating model fit. In addition, the RMSEA value indicated acceptable fit.

The standardized factor loadings and path coefficients are presented in Figure 6. All of the factor loadings were above .40. An examination of the path analyses demonstrates that all paths were significant at the p<.01 level except the direct effect of neighborhood on cardiovascular disease, which was significant at p<.05, and the direct effect of neighborhood on waist size, which was non-significant. The latent construct of neighborhood had a direct effect on the latent constructs of self-efficacy and physical activity as well as the outcome variables of self-rated health, BMI, and cardiovascular disease. More positive perceptions of the neighborhood context were associated with higher levels of self-efficacy (.175), greater physical activity (.088), and better health in regards to self-rated health (-.209) and BMI (-.056) and worse health in terms of cardiovascular disease (.030). The latent variable of self-efficacy evidenced a direct effect on physical activity, with higher levels of self-efficacy related to greater physical activity (.224). Finally, physical activity demonstrated a direct effect on all four health outcome variables, with greater physical activity related to better health outcomes (self-rated health: -.343; BMI: -.214; waist size: -.230; cardiovascular disease: -.251). As shown by the path coefficients, self-efficacy had a stronger direct relationship to physical activity than the neighborhood construct and physical activity had stronger direct relationships to each of the health outcome variables than neighborhood.

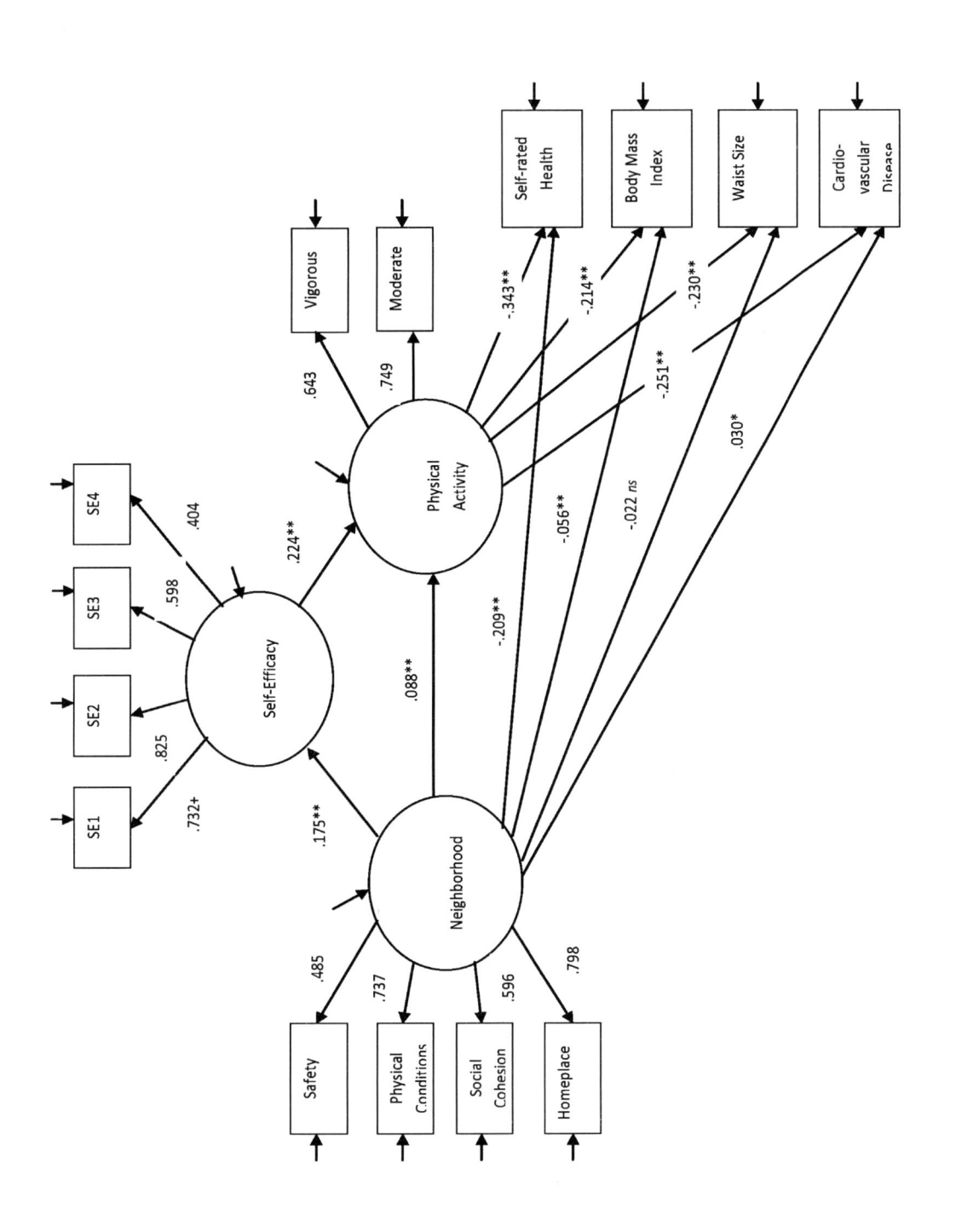

Figure 6. SEM results for Structural Model 1. Note: Path coefficients are standardized. += all factor loadings were .40 or higher; *= path statistically significant at the .05 level; **=path statistically significant at the .01 level; *ns*= path was not statistically significant. SE1= Self-efficacy 1: Keeping healthy depends on things that I can do; SE2= Self-efficacy 2: There are certain things I can do for myself to reduce the risk of a heart attack; SE3= Self-efficacy 3: There are certain things I can do for myself to reduce the risk of getting cancer; SE4= Self-efficacy 4: I work hard at trying to stay healthy.

Beyond the direct effects, the model hypothesized several indirect effects. All of these indirect effects were significant at the p<.01 level (values not shown in Figure 6 but presented in text). As hypothesized, the neighborhood environment had an indirect effect on physical activity through self-efficacy (.039). Furthermore, physical activity mediated the relationship between neighborhood and the outcome variables of self-rated health (-.030), BMI (-.019), waist size (-.020), and cardiovascular disease (-.022). As previously reported, neighborhood did not exert a direct effect on waist size; however, an indirect effect was found for this outcome variable. Overall, the model explained roughly 18% of the variance in self-rated health, 5% of the variance in BMI, 6% of the variance in waist size, and 6% of the variance in cardiovascular disease.

Structural Model 2

The second structural model hypothesized that 1. self-efficacy moderates the relationships between neighborhood and physical activity and 2. physical activity mediates the association between neighborhood and the health outcomes of self-rated health, body mass index, waist size, and cardiovascular disease. Two latent classes were created, high self-efficacy and low self-efficacy. The high self-efficacy group included 5,777 participants. The means of each of the self-efficacy items were high in this group (SE1= 5.48, SE2= 5.72, SE3= 4.96, SE4= 4.65). The low self-efficacy group included only 110 of the respondents and the means for each of the items were as follows: SE1= 1.54, SE2= 0.86, SE3= 1.42, SE4= 2.32. The overall model findings indicated model fit (N= 5782; χ^2= 347.40, df= 54, p<.001; CFI= .980; TLI= .967; RMSEA= .043); however, self-efficacy did not significantly moderate the relationship between neighborhood and physical activity (baseline χ^2= 347.40, df= 54; test χ^2= 348.20, df= 55; χ^2 difference

<3.84). Therefore, structural model 2 was not confirmed. Given that structural model 1 significantly fit the data and structural model 2 did not, demographic differences were tested in the first structural model.

Demographic Differences in Structural Model 1

The model was examined for differences based on the following demographic variables: age (young adulthood, early midlife, late midlife, and older adulthood), gender (males and females), ethnicity (whites and blacks), and education (did not graduate high school, graduated high school, some college, graduated college and beyond). The results are presented below.

To examine age differences, each age group (young adults: 20-34 years; early middle adults: 35-50 years; late midlife adults: 51-65 years; older adults: >65 years) combination was tested. Comparing young adults and early middle adults, one difference was found. The effect of neighborhood on physical activity was significant for early middle adults (standardized coefficient: .196, $p<.01$); however, it was not significant for young adults (standardized coefficient: .081, *ns*).

A greater number of differences were found between young adults and late midlife adults. The effect of neighborhood on physical activity was significant for late middle adults (.168, $p<.01$); however, it was not significant for young adults (.077, *ns*). In addition, the effect of physical activity on self-rated health was stronger for late midlife adults (-.419, $p<.01$) than young adults (-.224, $p<.01$). Finally, the effect of physical activity on cardiovascular disease was significant for late middle adults (-.181, $p<.01$) but was not significant for young adults (-.068, *ns*).

In examining the youngest and oldest age groups, four paths were significantly different. The magnitude of the effect of neighborhood on self-efficacy and on physical activity was greater for older adults (.186, $p<.01$; .190, $p<.01$, respectively) than young adults (.161, $p<.01$; .095, $p<.05$, respectively). Similarly, the effect of physical activity on waist size was greater in magnitude for older adults (-.180, $p<.01$) than young adults (-.170, $p<.01$). Furthermore, the standardized path coefficient between physical activity and cardiovascular disease was -.232 ($p<.01$) for older adults and .089 ($p<.05$) for young adults, demonstrating that the magnitude of the effect was larger for older adults.

One difference was evident between early middle adults and late middle adults. Specifically, the effect of physical activity on self-rated health was stronger for late midlife adults (-.402, $p<.01$) than for early midlife adults (-.311, $p<.01$).

The comparison of early middle adults and older adults revealed one significant path difference. The standardized coefficients for the path between physical activity and BMI were -.190 ($p<.01$) for early midlife adults and -.186 ($p<.01$) for older adults. Therefore, the effect of physical activity on BMI was greater in magnitude for early middle adults than older adults.

Only one path in the model was significantly different between late middle adults and older adults. While the path between self-efficacy and physical activity was significant at the $p<.01$ level for both age groups, the magnitude of the effect was greater for late middle adults (.217) than older adults (.162). Therefore, the effect of self-efficacy on physical activity was stronger for late middle adults.

The gender test evidenced differences in seven of the model's paths. First, the effect of neighborhood on physical activity differed. For males, the path was not significant (.022, *ns*). However, for females, the path was significant at the p<.01 level, with a standardized coefficient of .125. Second, the path between self-efficacy and physical activity differed by gender. Although the path was significant at the p<.01 level for both genders, the magnitude of the effect was greater for females (.252) than males (.131). In terms of the effect of neighborhood on the health outcomes, differences were evident for BMI and waist size. The effect of neighborhood on BMI was not significant for males (.014, *ns*); however, it was significant for females (-.100, p<.01). For the effect of neighborhood on waist size, the magnitude was greater for females (-.079, p<.01) than males (.052, p<.05). It should also be noted that the direction of the effect differed, with better neighborhood perceptions related to increased waist size for males. Finally, three differences were found for the effect of physical activity on the health outcomes. The effect of physical activity on self-rated health, BMI, and waist size was significant at the p<.01 level for both males and females. However, for all three of these paths, the magnitude of the effect was greater for females (self-rated health= males: -.302, females: -.331; BMI= males: -.125, females: -.274; waist size= males: -.228, females: -.339).

The comparison of whites and blacks demonstrated a significant difference in the effect of neighborhood on self-efficacy. Although the path was significant at the p<.01 level in both groups, the magnitude of the effect was larger for blacks than whites (standardized coefficients: .283 and .158, respectively). This suggests that the effect of neighborhood on self-efficacy was stronger for blacks than whites.

Finally, education differences were investigated. No differences were found between those who did not complete high school and those who completed high school. However, differences were found between all other education level combinations. The differences between those who did not complete high school and those with some college or college and beyond were evident in the paths between physical activity and health outcomes. For the path between physical activity and BMI, the effect was not significant for those who did not complete high school (-.089, *ns*) while it was significant for those with some college (-.269, p<.01). The path between physical activity and waist size also demonstrated a difference, with the magnitude of the effect greater for those with some college (-.296, p<.01) than those who did not complete high school (-.126, p<.05). In the comparison between those who did not complete high school and those with a college education and beyond, the effect of physical activity on cardiovascular disease was greater in magnitude for those who did not complete high school (-.313, p<.01; compared to college and beyond: -.159, p<.01).

Two significant path differences were evident between those who completed high school and those with some college. Specifically, the effect of physical activity on BMI was significant at the p<.01 level for both groups; however, the magnitude of the effect was greater for those with some college (-.271) than those who completed high school (-.172). A similar result was found for the path between physical activity and waist size, with a greater effect for those with some college (-.294, p<.01) than those who completed high school (-.179, p<.01).

Differences were also observed between those who completed high school and those with a college and beyond education level. For the path between neighborhood and self-efficacy, a greater magnitude was found for those with a high school education (.211, p<.01) than the college educated (.133, p<.01). In addition, an education difference was found in the relationship between neighborhood and BMI; however, this path was not significant for either education group (high school: -.045, *ns*; college and beyond: -.002, *ns*).

Finally, the comparisons between those who completed some college and those who completed college and beyond evidenced the greatest number of differences. The effect of neighborhood on BMI and on waist size was not significant for those with the highest education level (.011, *ns*, and .023, *ns*, respectively). However, for those who completed some college, neighborhood significantly impacted BMI (-.082, p<.01) and waist size (-.057, p<.05). The effect of physical activity on the health outcomes of BMI and cardiovascular disease also displayed education differences. The path between physical activity and BMI was significant at the p<.01 level for both those with some college experience and those who completed college; however, the magnitude of the effect was greater for those with some college education (-.236; compared to college and beyond: -.210). The same phenomenon was apparent in the relationship between physical activity and cardiovascular disease, with a stronger effect found for those with some college education (-.250, p<.01) than those with a college education and beyond (-.174, p<.01).

7. Discussion

The current study examined the relationships among the neighborhood/homeplace context, individual-level health-related self-efficacy, and health behaviors and outcomes. The results showed that self-efficacy served as a mediator in the relationship between context and health behaviors and that health behaviors mediated the neighborhood-health relationship. However, self-efficacy did not moderate the relationship between neighborhood/homeplace and health behaviors. Finally, an examination of demographic differences by age, gender, race, and education was conducted. A discussion of the results is presented, followed by the limitations of the research and conclusions.

The Latent Factors: Included and Excluded Variables

The neighborhood variables of perceived safety, physical conditions, social cohesion and homeplace informed the latent construct of neighborhood/homeplace. This finding supports the conceptualization that perceptions of all of these characteristics are vital to determining whether a neighborhood is healthy or unhealthy (Macintyre & Ellaway, 2000; Macintyre, Ellaway, & Cummins, 2002a; S. E. Taylor, et al., 1997). Contrary to expectations, the homeownership variable, an indicator of homeplace, did not load onto the latent factor. Several underlying forces may be at work in this result. First, while the items that loaded onto the factor were subjective evaluations of the quality of the context, the homeownership item was an objective measure of attachment to place. Reports have found that adults' subjective measurements of place are often more powerful predictors than objective measures (Ia Gory, Ward, & Sherman, 1985; Weden, Carpiano, & Robert, 2008; Wen, et al., 2006), which may explain the lack of significant loading across these two types of measurement. Second, while homeownership indicates a greater economic investment in the surrounding area, it does not necessarily imply perceived satisfaction with the context. It may be expected that homeownership in a neighborhood that is perceived poorly (resulting in the "trapping" effect of individuals' inability to relocate from a distressed area due to homeownership (White, 2001)) exacerbate the negative perceptions of place.

The items that were retained in the latent construct of self-efficacy and those that were rejected differed in wording in regards to an internal versus external focus. The retained items were more internally focused (e.g., "Keeping healthy depends on things that I can do"). However, the two items that did not load onto the factor were more externally driven. These include "When I am sick, getting better is in the doctor's hands" and "It is difficult for me to get good medical care". This difference in internal/external phrasing may impact the difference in factor loading. Furthermore, these latter two items may be largely confounded with other factors. For example, self-efficacy in the health domain does not infer the lack of medical attention. Attending regular health visits has been coined as a health-promoting behavior (Steptoe & Wardle, 2004). Therefore, seeking a doctor may be considered an efficacious behavior, especially when ill (with variation in the interpretation of "sick" likely across individuals). In addition, the receipt of good medical care may also be perceived as external to self-efficacy since it is largely impacted by the care available in the surrounding area as well as the participants' income and education level (Auchincloss, et al., 2001; Whitfield, et al., 2002).

Vigorous and moderate physical activity and smoking status were posited to contribute to the latent construct of health behaviors. However, smoking status did not load onto the factor and the construct was relabeled physical activity. One potential reason for this exclusion of smoking status may be the variability in the ex-smoker and current smoker groups. More specifically, smoking chronicity (e.g., length of time that the current smokers had been engaging in this behavior as well as both the length of time of smoking and length of time since smoking of the ex-smokers; number and frequency of cigarettes smoked) is not captured in the smoking status variable. These considerations may largely impact the congruence of the smoking status variable and physical activity items. Therefore, a more comprehensive smoking variable may be required for a latent construct of health behavior that also includes physical activity.

Originally, the health outcomes of self-rated health, obesity, and cardiovascular disease (including indicators of disease count and waist size) were hypothesized to map onto a latent factor. These items did not load onto a latent construct. Although each of the variables impacts the general notion of health, in creating such a large and dynamic construct as health, a much more inclusive set of indicators would likely be necessary. A future detailed investigation of various health indicators that map onto latent constructs of aspects of health is warranted.

Structural Model 1 Fit the Data

The potential mediating role of self-efficacy in the neighborhood-physical activity relationship has been suggested by previous research. In a study that examined changes in neighborhood satisfaction, self-efficacy, and physical activity over a 6-month period, Morris, McAuley, and Motl (2008) evidenced that changes in neighborhood satisfaction impacted changes in self-efficacy, which in turn were associated with increases in physical activity. In addition, McNeill, Wyrwich, and colleagues (2006) found that neighborhood quality was indirectly associated with physical activity through a path that included both intrinsic motivation and self-efficacy. While the former investigation did not explicitly assess the indirect effect of self-efficacy and the latter did not solely consider self-efficacy as a mediator (intrinsic motivation was included in the mediating path), both provide support for the mediating role of self-efficacy. Indeed, the current study found that health-related self-efficacy mediated the relationship between the neighborhood/homeplace context and physical activity.

A substantial amount of previous empirical evidence has demonstrated that the neighborhood environment impacts individuals' physical activity. As a selection, two investigations are further discussed (Addy, et al., 2004; Li, et al., 2005). Examining the physical conditions of street lighting and access to sidewalks as well as social cohesion, Addy and associates (2004) determined that these context variables were associated with physical activity. In a study of older adults, Li and colleagues (2005) identified neighborhood physical conditions and safety as significant predictors of walking. Moreover, physical activity is a known critical health-promoting behavior (Berlin & Colditz, 1990; Katzmarzyk, et al., 2003; Pate, et al., 1995; Steptoe & Wardle, 2004; U.S. Department of Health and Human Services, 1996). However, the potential mediating role of physical activity in the context-health relationship had not been tested. For example, while Poortinga (2006) examined the neighborhood environment, physical activity, self-rated health, and obesity, no mediation effects were investigated. Similarly, Ellaway, Macintyre, and Bonnefoy (2005) found that residential greenery was associated with increased physical activity and decreased obesity while the opposite was found for litter and graffiti; however, mediation was not tested. The present work also found that positive neighborhood perceptions were related to increased physical activity and that physical activity was significantly associated with health outcomes. Moving beyond the previous work, the additional step of mediation was tested and it was determined that physical activity mediated the link between neighborhood/homeplace and health outcomes.

Although previous work suggested that self-efficacy may serve as a mediator in the context- physical activity relationship and physical activity may mediate the impact of the neighborhood on health, the current study examined and empirically confirmed both of these mediating relationships. This finding is of importance because it underscores mechanisms by which the surrounding environment affects individual-level health variables, providing information concerning the ecology of health. Low levels of physical activity and health in some areas of the United States may be due to deteriorating neighborhood quality, which can be improved. For example, increased police presence, neighborhood watch, community events, aesthetics (clean and maintained streets and houses), and resource availability (e.g., walking trails, exercise facilities) may result in improved perceptions of safety, social cohesion, physical conditions, and homeplace, which in turn may translate into greater physical activity engagement. In connection with these efforts, self-efficacy can also be fostered through one or more of the six sources of self-efficacy development (i.e., mastery experiences, vicarious experiences, imaginal experiences, social persuasion, physiological arousal, and emotional states) (Bandura, 1977, 1986, 2000; Maddux, 1995). As an example, if individuals are provided with a mastery experience through tasks that they can personally achieve, their self-efficacy in the task will heighten. Therefore, understanding individuals' capabilities is critical in promoting a physical activity task that can be mastered (e.g., walking an appropriate distance). Mastery of the behavior may then increase their engagement in physical activity. Because the findings of this study demonstrate that neighborhood quality, self-efficacy, and physical activity operate in concert to impact health, promoting all three is expected to further strengthen intervention efforts.

Of note, all of the relationships within the model were in the expected direction except the direct link between neighborhood/homeplace and cardiovascular disease. Contrary to expectations, increased positive perceptions of neighborhood/homeplace were associated with increased cardiovascular disease morbidity. This result is in opposition to the previous research on neighborhoods and cardiovascular disease (Chaix, et al., 2008; Cohen, Farley, et al., 2003; Franzini & Spears, 2003; Kawachi, et al., 1997; Sundquist, et al., 2006) and small in magnitude; therefore, measurement differences are expected to underlie the divergent findings. Specifically, the previous studies utilized hospital records and death records, while the current study employed a self-report measure of cardiovascular disease.

The model indicates that physical activity exerted a greater direct effect on health outcomes than did the neighborhood variables. This finding points to the importance of policy that focuses on increasing physical activity. These efforts should also include variables that are known to impact physical activity and health. The present study helps to inform this discussion by showing that both the neighborhood environment and health-related self-efficacy are influential. Previous research has elucidated other key variables, such as motivation (Brownson, et al., 2001; McNeill, et al., 2006), the availability and quality of facilities for physical activity (Addy, et al., 2004; Booth, et al., 2000; Cleland, et al., 2008; Harrison, et al., 2007; Humpel, et al., 2002; Li, et al., 2005), and social support and the physical activity of others (Addy, et al., 2004; Booth, et al., 2000; Eyler, et al., 2003; Hooker, et al., 2005; King, et al., 2000; Wilbur, et al., 2003; Wilcox, et al., 2003). The further identification of the various influences and relative weight of these factors will be critical in determining the most effective and inclusive policy and intervention strategies that focus on physical activity in health improvement.

Self-efficacy Did Not Moderate the Neighborhood-Physical Activity Relationship

Self-efficacy did not serve as a moderator of the relationship between neighborhood/homeplace and physical activity; therefore, structural model 2 was rejected by the current data. One important consideration is the size of the two self-efficacy groups. A large majority of the sample (n= 5,777) was categorized in the high self-efficacy group, with only 110 participants included in the low self-efficacy group. While the fact that most individuals displayed high levels of self-efficacy is a positive finding in regards to adaptive personal competencies, it also limits the ability to test group differences and moderation. The minimum sample size required to run simple SEM models ranges from 100 to 150 (Hair, Black, Babin, Anderson, & Tatham, 2006), with more complex models requiring larger sample sizes. Therefore, the size of the low self-efficacy group was likely not sufficient for testing the current model. Given the theoretical and empirical support for the importance of self-efficacy for health behaviors, the lack of moderation may be influenced by the group size limitation. However, it is also possible that the strength of the impact of self-efficacy is not sufficient for moderating the effect of neighborhood on physical activity.

Demographic Differences Were Evident in Model 1
The Model Was Particularly Salient for Late Midlife and Older Adults

One of the primary goals of the current work was to examine age differences in the relationships among neighborhood/homplace, self-efficacy, and health behaviors and outcomes. For the most part, the age differences found suggest that these relationships are stronger for late middle age and older adults. As previously discussed, younger adults tend to spend less time in their neighborhood environment than middle aged and older adults (Cagney & Cornwell, in press; Glass & Balfour, 2003; Krantz-Kent & Stewart, 2007; Oh, 2003; Robinson & Godbey, 1997). Therefore, their physical activity and self-efficacy may be less influenced by this context. This difference in environmental exposure may provide some explanation for the age-related differences in the impact of neighborhood on physical activity and self-efficacy discovered in the current study. In addition to the differences in time spent in the neighborhood, the greater impact of neighborhood on self-efficacy for older adults in comparison to younger adults may point to the increased vulnerability and subsequent time required to adapt to the external environment with age, as hypothesized by Lawton (Lawton, 1982; Lawton & Nahemow, 1973). Also, because personal competencies such as self-efficacy may diminish with age, this provides the stage for external factors to exert a larger effect.

Interestingly, the link between health-related self-efficacy and physical activity was stronger for late middle adults than older adults. Competing factors begin to arise in older age and may even overshadow the impact of self-efficacy. For example, a longitudinal study of older adults determined that physical inactivity was associated with medical reasons, reduced walking speed, and living arrangements (Satariano, Haight, & Tager, 2000). The barrier of illness, injury, or disability may be particularly critical for older adults (Booth, Bauman, Owen, & Gore, 1997; Chinn, White, Harland, Drinkwater,

& Raybould, 1999; King, 2001; Satariano, et al., 2000), resulting in a lesser effect of self-efficacy in older adulthood than late middle adulthood. Although greater in late middle adulthood, the effect of self-efficacy was significant in older age, suggesting that this construct informs physical activity throughout the aging process.

For most of the age differences in the relationships between physical activity and health outcomes, the path was greater in magnitude for late middle adults and older adults compared to the two younger groups, with the exception of the impact of physical activity on BMI (with early middle adults showing a greater magnitude than older adults). In general, chronic conditions and age-related health decline escalate in late middle age and older age. For example, the percentage of the population with hypertension begins to exceed 50% in the 55-64 year age range and continues to increase with age (National Center for Health Statistics, 2009). Therefore, physical activity may have a stronger effect on health outcomes among these older populations because it serves to buffer against the perception and physical manifestation of health decline. One result did not show this pattern (the impact of physical activity on BMI). As demonstrated through national health statistics, obesity has a curvilinear relationship with age, with BMI increasing through middle adulthood and then decreasing in later life (National Center for Health Statistics, 2009). Decreases in weight and body mass over time are related to natural physical changes with age (Dey, Rothenberg, Sundh, Bosaeus, & Steen, 1999; Going, Williams, & Lohman, 1995; Launer & Harris, 1996; Perissinotto, Pisent, Sergi, Grigoletto, & Enzi, 2002) rather than changes due to physical activity. This may partially explain the finding that the impact of physical activity on BMI is stronger for early midlife adults than older adults.

Greater Impacts Were Found for Females

The examination of gender revealed that the model was particularly salient for females. In fact, all of the significant gender differences evidenced a greater magnitude of the effect for females. The items that were used to measure neighborhood/homeplace in the current work may be disproportionately pertinent for females. Research has shown that neighborhood factors differentially impact men and women. As previously mentioned, in a study of older adults in Norway, Piro, Noess, and Claussen (2006) discovered that objectively measured neighborhood violence had an impact on males and subjective perceptions of neighborhood safety impacted females. The current study included only subjective measures of neighborhood, which may have influenced the gender differences found. However, it is also possible that the effect of the neighborhood/homeplace environment is more substantial for females. A study of fear of crime supports this notion as females displayed greater perceived risk and fear of crime than males regardless of the measurement utilized (LaGrange & Ferraro, 1989). In addition, Shenk and colleagues (2004) suggest that gender differences in the relation to homeplace may be due to gender roles and expectations, especially when considering older women in the United States as traditional gender roles were emphasized in the upbringing of these older cohorts.

In considering the gender differences in the relationship between self-efficacy and physical activity, investigations of gender disparities in reasons or motivations for physical activity were identified. Although various differences have been found, self-efficacy does not appear to be a gender-differentiating variable. In a study on the adoption and maintenance of vigorous physical activity, Sallis and associates (1992) found that self-efficacy predicted change in activity over time in sedentary men and women and that the levels of self-efficacy were similar. Comparing active men and women, self-efficacy was a significant predictor for men but not women (Sallis, et al., 1992). It should be noted that this study measured exercise-specific self-efficacy while the current study measured health-related self-efficacy. Therefore, further study of the gender differences in the relation between self-efficacy and physical activity should compare various types of self-efficacy that are associated with physical activity as well as how these may vary based on the type of physical activity engagement. A greater understanding of these associations may aid in promoting physical activity. Given that women engage in less physical activity than men, knowledge of the gender differences in reasons and motivations for physical activity is especially important for efforts that target women.

The current model demonstrated that the effect of physical activity on the health outcomes of self-rated health, BMI, and waist size was greater in magnitude for females. Although there was a significant difference for self-rated health, it was small in magnitude. Women are more likely than men to state weight control as a motivation for physical activity (McDonald & Thompson, 1992; Silberstein, Striegel-Moore, Timko, & Rodin, 1988; Tiggemann & Williamson, 2000). As noted, physical activity significantly impacted BMI and waist size. These findings may be interrelated such that because physical activity was associated with measures related to weight control, a primary concern for women, it also exhibited a greater impact on females' perceptions of health due to the salience of the goal of weight control. The discussion of gender disparities in the effect of physical activity on BMI and waist size requires a consideration of the physical differences of men and women. Gender differences in body fat include a high percentage in women as well as differing areas of fat storage (Blaak, 2001). Interestingly, differences in the energy derived from fat during physical activity favors women (Blaak, 2001). This result may partially explain the greater impact of physical activity on the outcomes of BMI and waist size for women.

The Influence of Neighborhood on Self-efficacy Was Greater for Blacks

Blacks are more likely to reside in neighborhoods with fewer resources than whites (Evans & Kantrowitz, 2002; Leventhal & Brooks-Gunn, 2000; Rosenbaum & Harris, 2001). Therefore, the more limited access to resources, such as health facilities, may partially explain the greater impact of neighborhood/homeplace on health-related self-efficacy among blacks. For example, fewer health resources may lead to lesser knowledge and/or greater confusion concerning health matters, resulting in a greater impact of the environment on health-related self-efficacy. Given the consistently observed disparities between blacks and whites, identifying and intervening in processes in which blacks may be at a disadvantage is critical. Therefore, the current finding proposes that a deeper understanding of the relationship between the context and self-efficacy among blacks is necessary.

Education

Lower education is associated with less access to medical care, less health knowledge, and less adaptive doctor-patient communication (Cotugna, Subar, Heimendinger, & Kahle, 1992; DeWalt, Berkman, Sheridan, Lohr, & Pignone, 2004; Fiscella, Franks, Gold, & Clancy, 2000; Willems, De Maesschalck, Deveugele, Derese, & De Maeseneer, 2005). These factors may, in turn, translate into a greater impact of the external environment on health-related self-efficacy, as was found in the current study. Specifically, the magnitude of the effect of neighborhood on self-efficacy was stronger for those who completed high school than those who completed college.

For the significant path differences that included health outcomes, the impact of the model paths was especially prominent for those with some college experience but no college degree. The effect of neighborhood on BMI and waist size was greater in magnitude for those who attended some college than those who completed a college degree. A possible explanation for this effect is that these health factors may be impacted by the work environment to a greater extent among those who received a college degree or higher. Those who achieve higher education degrees are more likely to become employed in a higher social status occupation (for example, see Pascarella & Terenzini, 2005). This type of work environment may promote health due to the greater education and health knowledge of the employees. Given that the work environment was not examined in the current study, future research should further investigate the impact of the workplace on health outcomes.

Increases in education are associated with increased knowledge of the exercise recommendations as well as the relationship between physical activity engagement and health (Kenkel, 1991; Morrow Jr., Krzewinski-Malone, Jackson, Bungum, & FizGerald, 2004). This may provide insight into the significant differences between those with some college and those with less education in the paths between physical activity and the health outcomes of BMI and waist size. However, the magnitude of the effect of physical activity on BMI and cardiovascular disease was greater for those with some college education than those who completed a college education and beyond. Considering these comparisons, it is possible that additional factors become increasingly salient with higher education. For example, those with higher education receive higher quality health care (Barr, 2008; Davis, et al., 2007; Fiscella, et al., 2000), which may result in the slightly lower impact of physical activity (when compared to those with some college).

Given that lower education is associated with decreased access and quality of health care as well as health and physical activity knowledge, programs that promote health education, patient-doctor communication, and service access should be made more widely available to those with lower education attainment.

Limitations

Several limitations of the current project should be noted. First, secondary data analysis was used. Secondary data often limits the scope of investigation as the variables that are collected as well as the collection methods are determined by the study's principal investigators rather than the secondary researcher. However, the use of the MIDUS dataset allowed for a large-scale national examination of the study hypotheses across adulthood, which would otherwise not have been feasible, minimizing the limitations associated with the use of secondary data.

Second, all of the data was based on self-report items. This includes the physical variables of height and weight, which were used to determine BMI, as well as waist size. The participants measured and reported these variables. With all self-report data, there is the possibility of misreporting as well as reporter bias. However, given the nature of the study, many of the constructs require self-report (e.g., neighborhood perceptions, self-efficacy, and self-rated health). Objective measures of neighborhood include crime statistics, number of dilapidated buildings, and presence of community resources and organizations. To objectively measure physical activity, heart rate monitors and pedometers or step counters could be used. A more objective approach (e.g., medical reports) to the physical health variables would have provided valuable insight by offering a direct measure of health; therefore, future research should incorporate not only subjective, but also objective measures of physical health variables.

As mentioned, neighborhood perception was collected through self-report; however, the participants' definition of their neighborhood was not assessed. Therefore, the area of consideration could widely vary (e.g., a neighborhood definition of a few streets vs. a definition of an entire city). This potential inconsistency in neighborhood definition could influence the results. However, individuals likely define their neighborhoods based on the areas that are most relevant to them, which may similarly impact health regardless of the size of the reported area. Even with this consideration, future research should capture participants' definition of neighborhood in order to obtain richer data on the area of interest and determine whether results vary based on the definition of the neighborhood.

Furthermore, the study is limited in its generalizability to the oldest segments of the population. Although the current sample included a wide age range of adults (20-75 years), the addition of individuals above the age of 75 would have provided further insight into the association of contextual, individual, and health differences with aging. The investigation of future waves of MIDUS will be informative in testing not only change over time, but also the significance of the present findings among those in the very late years.

Finally, the vast difference in the number of whites and blacks in the sample limited the ability to perform an in-depth examination of racial differences. While an additional minority sample was collected, the measurement differed such that the minority sample could not be included in the analyses. Although a more thorough examination of black/white differences would potentially shed light onto the known health disparities between these groups, this was not the primary goal of the study. As a secondary consideration, the investigation of racial differences that was possible was adequate. However, future research should aim to target racial minority groups, especially given the demographic changes of the United States (with the rapidly increasing racial minority populations).

Although the current study is affected by the abovementioned limitations, it is the first to investigate both the mediating effects of self-efficacy and physical activity in the relationship between neighborhood and health outcomes across a U.S. sample of adults. The results demonstrate that neighborhood not only impacts health, but also influences several other individual-level constructs, which in turn play a role in the relationship between neighborhood and health. Therefore, the findings are an important step in understanding the dynamic and complex interrelations between context, individual factors, and health and a springboard for future research on the area.

8. Conclusion

Based on the theoretical work of M. Powell Lawton, Thomas Glass, and Jennifer Balfour as well as previous empirical studies, the current work examined the interrelationships among the neighborhood/homeplace context, self-efficacy, physical activity, and health outcomes. The results supported a model that includes two mediating relationships: 1. health-related self-efficacy mediated the relationship between neighborhood/homeplace and physical activity and 2. physical activity served as a mediator between the neighborhood environment and health outcomes. In addition, demographic differences indicated that the model was most salient for those in the late midlife and older ages, females, blacks, and those with some college experience.

Given these findings as well as the limitations of the study, several suggestions are provided for future research. First, in regards to research populations, investigations should target minority populations in order to test underlying mechanisms of health disparities by racial group. Furthermore, data should be gathered to include the full range of adult ages. The participants of the present study were 20-75 years old; therefore, those in the oldest ages were not represented. Given that both physical activity and health decline with increasing age, these older individuals must be considered in order to fully test aging effects.

Measurement should incorporate not only subjective, but also objective measures of neighborhood, physical activity, and health outcomes. This will aid in minimizing rater bias as well as provide a more comprehensive view of the constructs and their interactions. In addition, various measures of self-efficacy should be examined, including those specific to physical activity engagement. Given that physical activity had the greatest direct effect on health in the model, additional variables that impact physical activity should be investigated in terms of their significance and relative weight. Furthermore, various contexts may have differential impacts on individuals based on age, education, and other demographic variables. Therefore, the inclusion of other contexts, such as the workplace, would be beneficial to future research.

Several areas of policy and intervention focus were also indicated by the present work. Given that neighborhood, self-efficacy, and physical activity operate in concert to impact health outcomes, intervening at each of these levels will likely result in the greatest health improvements. Some recommendations include increasing neighborhood police presence, neighborhood watch, aesthetics, and resources in an effort to improve neighborhood quality. Self-efficacy can be increased through methods such as mastery experiences of achievable physical activity behaviors and vicarious experiences of observing social models achieve adaptive behaviors. These methods also directly and indirectly increase physical activity. As physical activity has the largest direct effect on health, further research should particularly focus on gaining knowledge of the barriers and motivations for physical activity and promoting activity.

Overall, the work in this study contributes to the knowledge of person-environment relationships and aging by demonstrating the interrelations among neighborhood, self-efficacy, physical activity, and health as well as the discovery of changes in these relationships with age. The results contained herein suggest that physical activity should be targeted in efforts to improve health, especially for older adults and women. In so doing, factors that impact physical activity engagement, including the neighborhood context and self-efficacy (among others), should also be further considered. This will result in more ecological and complete policies and interventions that aim to improve health.

References

Addy, C. L., Wilson, D. K., Kirtland, K. A., Ainsworth, B. E., Sharpe, P., & Kimsey, D. (2004). Associations of perceived social and physical environmental supports with physical activity and walking behavior. *American Journal of Public Health, 94*, 440-443.

Adler, N. E. (2006). Overview of health disparities. In G. E. Thompson, F. Mitchell & M. Williams (Eds.), *Examining the Health Disparities Research Plan of the National Institutes of Health: Unfinished Business* (pp. 129-188). Washington, DC: National Academic Press.

Adler, N. E. (2009). Health disparities through a psychological lens. *American Psychologist, 64*, 663-673.

Anastasi, A. (1958). Heredity, environment, and the question "How?". *Psychological Review, 65*, 197-208.

Anderson, J. C., & Gerbing, D. W. (1988). Structural equation modeling in practice: A review and recommended two-step approach. *Psychological Bulletin, 103*, 411-423.

Angel, J. L., & Hogan, D. P. (1992). The demography of minority aging populations. *Journal of Family History, 17*, 95-115.

Arnett, J. (2006). Emerging adulthood: Understanding the new way of coming of age. In J. Arnett & J. Tanner (Eds.), *Emerging Adults in America: Coming of Age in the 21st Century* (pp. 3-19). Washington, DC: American Psychological Association.

Arras, R. E., Ogletree, R. J., & Welshimer, K. J. (2006). Health-promoting behaviors in men age 45 and above. *International Journal of Men's Health, 5*, 65-79.

Atchley, R. (2000). *Social Forces and Aging: Creating Positive Experiences*. Belmont, CA: Wadsworth.

Auchincloss, A. H., Van Nostrand, J. F., & Ronsaville, D. (2001). Access to health care for older persons in the United States: Personal, structural, and neighborhood characteristics. *Journal of Aging and Health, 13*, 329-354.

Avis, N. E. (1999). Women's health at midlife. In S. L. Willis & J. D. Reid (Eds.), *Life in the Middle: Psychological and Social Development in Middle Age* (pp. 105-146). San Diego, CA: Academic Press.

Baltes, P. B., & Smith, J. (1990). Toward a psychology of wisdom and its ontogenesis. In R. J. Sternberg (Ed.), *Wisdom: Its Nature, Origins, and Development* (pp. 87-120). Cambridge, England: Cambridge University Press.

Bandura, A. (1977). Self-efficacy: Toward a unifying theory of behavioral change. *Psychological Review, 84*, 191-215.

Bandura, A. (1986). *Social Foundations of Thought and Action: A Social Cognitive Theory*. Englewood Cliffs, NJ: Prentice-Hall, Inc.

Bandura, A. (1989). Human agency in social cognitive theory. *American Psychologist, 44*, 1175-1184.

Bandura, A. (1990). Some reflections on reflections. *Psychological Inquiry, 1*, 101-105.

Bandura, A. (1997). *Self-efficacy: The Exercise of Control*. New York, NY: W.H. Freeman and Company.

Bandura, A. (2000). Health promotion from the perspective of social cognitive theory. In P. Norman, C. Abraham & M. Conner (Eds.), *Understanding and Changing Health Behaviour: From Health Beliefs to Self-regulation* (pp. 299-339). Amsterdam, The Netherlands: Harwood Academic Publishers.

Barr, D. A. (2008). *Health Disparities in the United States: Social Class, Race, Ethnicity, and Health*. Baltimore, MD: Johns Hopkins University Press.

Bentler, P. M. (1989). *EQS Structural Equations Program Manual*. Los Angeles, CA: BMDP Statistical Software.

Bentler, P. M. (1990). Comparative fit indices in structural models. *Psychological Bulletin, 107*, 238-246.

Berg, C. J., Sanderson Cox, L., Mahnken, J. D., Greiner, K. A., & Ellerbeck, E. F. (2008). Correlates of self-efficacy among rural smokers. *Journal of Health Psychology, 13*, 416-421.

Berlin, J. A., & Colditz, G. A. (1990). A meta-analysis of physical activity in the prevention of coronary heart disease. *American Journal of Epidemiology, 132*, 639-636.

Blaak, E. (2001). Gender differences in fat metabolism. *Current Opinion in Clinical Nutrition and Metabolic Care, 4*, 499-502.

Black, J. L., & Macinko, J. (2008). Neighborhoods and obesity. *Nutrition Reviews, 66*, 2-20.

Boardman, T., Catley, D., Mayo, M. S., & Ahluwalia, J. S. (2005). Self-efficacy and motivation to quit during participation in a smoking cessation program. *International Journal of Behavioral Medicine, 12*, 266-272.

Bollen, K. A. (1989). *Structural Equations with Latent Variables*. New York, NY: Wiley.

Booth, M. L., Bauman, A., Owen, N., & Gore, C. J. (1997). Physical activity preferences, preferred sources of assistance, and perceived barriers to increased activity among physically inactive Australians. *Preventive Medicine, 26*, 131-137.

Booth, M. L., Owen, N., Bauman, A., Clavisi, O., & Leslie, E. (2000). Social-cognitive and perceived environment influences associated with physical activity in older Australians. *Preventive Medicine, 31*, 15-22.

Brondolo, E., Rieppi, R., Kelly, K. P., & Gerin, W. (2003). Perceived racism and blood pressure: A review of the literature and conceptual and methodological critique. *Annals of Behavioral Medicine, 25*, 55-65.

Bronfenbrenner, U. (1977). Toward an experimental ecology of human development. *American Psychologist, 32*, 513-530.

Bronfenbrenner, U. (1979). *The Ecology of Human Development: Experiments by Nature and Design*. Cambridge, MA: Harvard University Press.

Bronfenbrenner, U. (1989). Ecological systems theory. In R. Vasta (Ed.), *Annals of Child Development* (Vol. 6, pp. 187-249). Greenwich, CT: JAI.

Browne, M. W., & Cudeck, R. (1990). Single sample cross-validation indices for covariance structures. *Multivariate Behavioral Research, 24*, 445-455.

Brownson, R. C., Baker, E. A., Housemann, R. A., Brennan, L. K., & Bacak, S. J. (2001). Environmental and policy determinants of physical activity in the United States. *American Journal of Public Health, 91*, 1995-2003.

Bulatao, R. A., & Anderson, N. B. (Eds.). (2004). *Understanding Racial and Ethnic Differences in Health in Late Life: A Research Agenda*. Washington, DC: The National Academies Press.

Burdette, H. L., Wadden, T. A., & Whitaker, R. C. (2006). Neighborhood safety, collective efficacy, and obesity in women with young children. *Obesity, 14*, 518-525.

Bursik Jr., R. J., & Grasmick, H. G. (1993). *Neighborhoods and crime: The dimensions of effective community control*. New York, NY: Lexington Books.

Burton, L. M., & Lawson Clark, S. (2005). Homeplace and housing in the lives of low-income urban African American families. In V. C. McLoyd, N. E. Hill & K. A. Dodge (Eds.), *African American Family Life: Ecological and Cultural Diversity* (pp. 166-188). New York, NY: The Guilford Press.

Burton, L. M., Win, D. M., Stevenson, H., & Lawson Clark, S. (2004). Working with African American clients: Considering the "homeplace" in marriage and family therapy practices. *Journal of Marriage and Family Therapy, 30*, 397-410.

Cagney, K. A., & Cornwell, E. Y. (in press). Neighborhoods and health. *Annual Reviews of Geriatrics and Gerontology*.

Casey, A. A., Elliott, M., Glanz, K., Haire-Joshu, D., Lovegreen, S. L., Saelens, B. E., et al. (2008). Impact of the food environment and physical activity environment on behaviors and weight status in rural U.S. communities. *Preventive Medicine, 47*, 600-604.

Centers for Disease Control and Prevention Health Effects of Cigarette Smoking. Retrieved January 10, 2010: http://www.cdc.gov/tobacco/data_statistics/fact_sheets/health_effects/effects_cig_smoking/index.htm

Chaix, B., Lindstrom, M., Rosvall, M., & Merlo, J. (2008). Neighbourhood social interactions and risk of acute myocardial infarction. *Journal of Epidemiology & Community Health, 62*, 62-68.

Chandola, T. (2001). The fear of crime and area differences in health. *Health & Place, 7*, 105-116.

Chinn, D. J., White, M., Harland, J., Drinkwater, C., & Raybould, S. (1999). Barriers to physical activity and socioeconomic position: Implications for health promotion. *Journal of Epidemiology & Community Health, 53*, 191-192.

Cleland, V. J., Timperio, A., & Crawford, D. (2008). Are perceptions of the physical and social environment associated with mothers' walking for leisure and for transport? A longitudinal study. *Preventive Medicine, 47*, 188-193.

Cohen, D. A., Farley, T. A., & Mason, K. (2003). Why is poverty unhealthy? Social and physical mediators. *Social Science & Medicine, 57*, 1631-1641.

Cohen, D. A., Mason, K., Bedimo, A., Scribner, R., Basolo, V., & Farley, T. A. (2003). Neighborhood physical conditions and health. *American Journal of Public Health, 93*, 467-471.

Conner, M., & Norman, P. (1996). The role of social cognition in health behaviours. In M. Conner & P. Norman (Eds.), *Predicitng Health Behaviour: Research and Practice with Social Cognition Models* (pp. 1-22). Bristol, PA: Open University Press.

Cotugna, N., Subar, A. F., Heimendinger, J., & Kahle, L. (1992). Nutrition and cancer prevention knowledge, beliefs, attitudes, and practices: The 1987 National Health Interview Survey. *Journal of the American Dietetic Association, 92*, 963-968.

Cummins, S., Stafford, M., Macintyre, S., Marmot, M., & Ellaway, A. (2005). Neighbourhood environment and its association with self rated health: Evidence from Scotland and England. *Journal of Epidemiology & Community Health, 59*, 207-213.

Daviglus, M. L., Liu, K., Yan, L. L., Pirzada, A., Manheim, L., Manning, W., et al. (2004). Relation of body mass index in young adulthood and middle age to Medicare expenditures in older age. *Journal of the American Medical Association, 292*, 2743-2749.

Davis, A. M., Vinci, L. M., Okwuosa, T. M., Chase, A. R., & Huang, E. S. (2007). Cardiovascular health disparities: A systematic review of health care interventions. *Medical Care Research and Review, 64*(5 Suppl.), 29S-100S.

de Koning, L., Merchant, A. T., Pogue, J., & Anand, S. S. (2007). Waist circumference and waist-to-hip ratio as predictors of cardiovascular events: Meta-regression analysis of prospective studies. *European Heart Journal, 28*, 850-856.

DeWalt, D. A., Berkman, N. D., Sheridan, S., Lohr, K. N., & Pignone, M. P. (2004). Literacy and health outcomes: A systematic review of the literature. *Journal of General Internal Medicine, 19*, 1228-1239.

Dey, D. K., Rothenberg, E., Sundh, V., Bosaeus, I., & Steen, B. (1999). Height and body weight in the elderly. I. A 25 year longitudinal study of a population aged 70 to 95 years. *European Journal of Clinical Nutrition, 53*, 905-914.

Dressler, W. W., Oths, K. S., & Gravlee, C. C. (2005). Race and ethnicity in public health research: Models to explain health disparities. *Annual Review of Anthropology, 34*, 231-252.

Duncan, M., & Mummery, K. (2005). Psychosocial and environmental factors associated with physical activity among city dwellers in regional Queensland. *Preventive Medicine, 40*, 363-372.

Echeverria, S., Diez-Roux, A. V., Shea, S., Borrell, L. N., & Jackson, S. (2008). Associations of neighborhood problems and neighborhood social cohesion with mental health and health behaviors: The Multi-Ethnic Study of Atherosclerosis. *Health & Place, 14*, 853-865.

Ellaway, A., Macintyre, S., & Bonnefoy, X. (2005). Graffiti, greenery, and obesity in adults: Secondary analysis of European cross sectional survey. *British Medical Journal, 331*, 611-612.

Ellaway, A., Macintyre, S., & Kearns, A. (2001). Perceptions of place and health in socially contrasting neighbourhoods. *Urban Studies, 38*, 2299-2316.

Evans, G. W., & Kantrowitz, E. (2002). Socioeconomic status and health: The potential role of environmental risk exposure. *Annual Review of Public Health, 23*, 303-331.

Eyler, A. A., Baker, E., Cromer, L., King, A. C., Brownson, R. C., & Donatelle, R. J. (1998). Physical activity and minority women: A qualitative study. *Health Education & Behavior, 25*, 640-652.

Eyler, A. A., Matson-Koffman, D., Young, D. R., Wilcox, S., Wilbur, J., Thompson, J. L., et al. (2003). Quantitative study of correlates of physical activity in women from diverse racial/ethnic groups: The Women's Cardiovascular Health Network Project summary and conclusions. *American Journal of Preventive Medicine, 25*(3 Suppl. 1), 93-103.

Fayers, P. M., & Sprangers, M. A. (2002). Understanding self-rated health. *Lancet, 359*, 187-188.

Ferguson, K. M., & Mindel, C. H. (2007). Modeling fear of crime in Dallas neighborhoods: A test of social capital theory. *Crime & Delinquency, 53*, 322-349.

Ferraro, K. F. (2006). Health and aging. In R. H. Binstock & L. K. George (Eds.), *Handbook of Aging and the Social Sciences* (6th ed., pp. 238-256). San Diego, CA: Academic Press.

Ferron, J. M., & Hess, M. R. (2007). Estimation in SEM: A concrete example. *Journal of Educational and Behavioral Statistics, 32*, 110-120.

Fiscella, K., Franks, P., Gold, M. R., & Clancy, C. M. (2000). Inequality in quality: Addressing socioeconomic, racial, and ethnic disparities in health care. *Journal of the American Medical Association, 283*, 2579-2584.

Fisher, J. (1993). A framework for describing developmental change among older adults. *Adult Education Quarterly, 43*, 76-89.

Flegal, K. M. (2005). Epidemiologic aspects of overweight and obesity in the United States. *Physiology & Behavior, 86*, 599-602.

Flegal, K. M., Troiano, R. P., Pamuk, E. R., Kuczmarski, R. J., & Campbell, S. M. (1995). The influence of smoking cessation on the prevalence of overweight in the United States. *New England Journal of Medicine, 333*, 1165-1170.

Foster, C., Hillsdon, M., & Thorogood, M. (2004). Environmental perceptions and walking in English adults. *Journal of Epidemiology & Community Health, 58*, 924-928.

Franzini, L., Caughy, M., Spears, W., & Fernandez Esquer, M. E. (2005). Neighborhood economic conditions, social processes, and self-rated health in low-income neighborhoods in Texas: A multilevel latent variables model. *Social Science & Medicine, 61*, 1135-1150.

Franzini, L., & Spears, W. (2003). Contributions of social context to inequalities in years of life lost to heart disease in Texas, USA. *Social Science & Medicine, 57*, 1847-1861.

Fullilove, M. T., & Fullilove III, R. E. (2000). What's housing got to do with it? *American Journal of Public Health, 90*, 183-184.

Ganz, M. (2000). The relationship between external threats and smoking in central Harlem. *American Journal of Public Health, 90*, 367-371.

Garcia, K., & Mann, T. (2003). From 'I wish' to 'I will': Social-cognitive predictors of behavioral intentions. *Journal of Health Psychology, 8*, 347-360.

Geldmacher, D. S. (2009). Alzheimer disease. In M. F. Weiner & A. M. Lipton (Eds.), *The American Psychiatric Publishing Textbook of Alzheimer Disease and Other Dementias* (pp. 155-172). Arlington, VA: American Psychiatric Publishing, Inc.

Gitlin, L. N. (2003). Conducting research on home environments: Lessons learned and new directions. *The Gerontologist, 43*, 628-637.

Glass, T. A., & Balfour, J. L. (2003). Neighborhoods, aging, and functional limitations. In I. Kawachi & L. F. Berkman (Eds.), *Neighborhoods and Health* (pp. 303-334). New York, NY: Oxford University Press.

Going, S., Williams, D., & Lohman, T. (1995). Aging and body composition: Biological changes and methodological issues. *Exercise and Sport Sciences Review, 23*, 411-458.

Gottlieb, G. (1998). Normally occurring environmental and behavioral influences on gene activity: From central dogma to probabilistic epigenesis. *Psychological Review, 105*, 792-802.

Gottlieb, G. (2000). Environmental and behavioral influences on gene activity. *Current Directions in Psychological Science, 9*, 93-97.

Gwaltney, C. J., Metrik, J., Kahler, C. W., & Shiffman, S. (2009). Self-efficacy and smoking cessation: A meta-analysis. *Psychology of Addictive Behaviors, 23*, 56-66.

Gwaltney, C. J., Shiffman, S., Balabanis, M. H., & Paty, J. A. (2005). Dynamic self-efficacy outcome expectancies: Prediction of smoking lapse and relapse. *Journal of Abnormal Psychology, 114*, 661-675.

Hair, J. F., Black, B., Babin, B., Anderson, R. E., & Tatham, R. L. (2006). *Multivariate Data Analysis* (6th ed.). Englewood Cliffs, NJ: Prentice Hall.

Hansson, R. O., & Carpenter, B. N. (1994). *Relationships in Old Age: Coping with the Challenge of Transition*. New York, NY: The Guilford Press.

Harrison, R. A., Gemmell, I., & Heller, R. F. (2007). The population effect of crime and neighbourhood on physical activity: An analysis of 15 461 adults. *Journal of Epidemiology & Community Health, 61*, 34-39.

Heron, M. P., Hoyert, D. L., Murphy, S. L., Xu, J. Q., Kochanek, K. D., & Tejada-Vera, B. (2009). Deaths: Final data for 2006 *National Vital Statistics Reports* (Vol. 57, pp. 1-135). Hyattsville, MD: National Center for Health Statistics.

Hooker, S. P., Wilson, D. K., Griffin, S. F., & Ainsworth, B. E. (2005). Perceptions of environmental supports for physical activity in African American and White adults in a rural county in South Carolina. *Preventing Chronic Disease, 2*(4), 1-10.

Hoyle, R. H. (Ed.). (1995). *Structural Equation Modeling: Concepts, Issues, and Applications*. Thousand Oaks, CA: Sage Publications.

Hoyle, R. H., & Panter, A. T. (1995). Writing about structural equation models. In R. H. Hoyle (Ed.), *Structural Equation Modeling: Concepts, Issues, and Applications* (pp. 158-176). Thousand Oaks, CA: Sage Publications.

Hu, L., & Bentler, P. M. (1995). Evaluating model fit. In R. H. Hoyle (Ed.), *Structural Equation Modeling: Concepts, Issues, and Applications* (pp. 76-99). Thousand Oaks, CA: Sage Publications.

Humpel, N., Owen, N., & Leslie, E. (2002). Environmental factors associated with adults' participation in physical activity: A review. *American Journal of Preventive Medicine, 22*, 188-199.

Ia Gory, M., Ward, R., & Sherman, S. (1985). The ecology of aging: Neighborhood satisfaction in an older adult population. *The Sociological Quarterly, 26*, 405-418.

Idler, E. L., & Angel, R. J. (1990). Self-rated health and mortality in the NHANES-I epidemiologic follow-up study. *American Journal of Public Health, 80*, 446-452.

Idler, E. L., & Benyamini, Y. (1997). Self-rated health and mortality: A review of twenty-seven community studies. *Journal of Health and Social Behavior, 38*, 21-37.

Idler, E. L., Russell, L. B., & Davis, D. (2000). Survival, functional limitations, and self-rated health in the NHANES-I epidemiologic follow-up study. *American Journal of Epidemiology, 152*, 874-883.

International Agency for Research on Cancer (2002). *IARC Handbooks of Cancer Prevention, Vol. 6: Weight Control and Physical Activity*. Washington, DC: IARC Press.

Jeffords, C. R. (1983). The situational relationship between age and the fear of crime. *International Journal of Aging and Human Development, 17*, 103-111.

Katzmarzyk, P. T., Janssen, I., & Ardern, C. I. (2003). Physical inactivity, excess adiposity and premature mortality. *Obesity Reviews, 4*, 257-290.

Kawachi, I., & Berkman, L. F. (2000). Social cohesion, social capital, and health. In L. F. Berkman & I. Kawachi (Eds.), *Social Epidemiology* (pp. 174-190). New York, NY: Oxford University Press.

Kawachi, I., Kennedy, B. P., & Glass, R. (1999). Social capital and self-rated health: A contextual analysis. *American Journal of Public Health, 89*, 1187-1193.

Kawachi, I., Kennedy, B. P., Lochner, K., & Prothrow-Stith, D. (1997). Social capital, income inequality, and mortality. *American Journal of Public Health, 87*, 1491-1498.

Kenkel, D. S. (1991). Health behavior, health knowledge, and schooling. *Journal of Political Economy, 99*, 287-305.

Keyes, C. L. M. (1998). Social well-being. *Social Psychology Quarterly, 61*, 121-137.

King, A. C. (2001). Interventions to promote physical activity in older adults. *The Journals of Gerontology: Series A: Biological Sciences and Medical Sciences 56 (suppl. 2)*, 36-46.

King, A. C., Castro, C., Wilcox, S., Eyler, A. A., Sallis, J. F., & Brownson, R. C. (2000). Personal and environmental factors associated with physical inactivity among different racial-ethnic groups of U.S. middle-aged and older-aged women. *Health Psychology, 19*, 354-364.

Kline, R. B. (Ed.). (2005). *Principles and Practice of Structural Equation Modeling* (2nd ed.). New York, NY: The Guilford Press.

Kolb, P. J. (2008). Developmental theories of aging. In S. G. Austrian (Ed.), *Developmental Theories Through the Life Cycle* (2nd ed., pp. 285-364). New York, NY: Columbia University Press.

Konstam, V. (2007). *Emerging and Young Adulthood: Multiple Perspectives, Diverse Narratives*. New York, NY: Springer.

Krantz-Kent, R., & Stewart, J. (2007). How do older Americans spend their time? *Monthly Labor Review, 130*, 8-26.

Krause, N. (1996). Neighborhood deterioration and self-rated health in later life. *Psychology and Aging, 11*, 342-352.

Krause, N. (1998). Neighborhood deterioration, religious coping, and changes in health during late life. *The Gerontologist, 38*, 653-664.

Lachman, M. E., & James, J. B. (1997). Charting the course of midlife development: An overview. In M. E. Lachman & J. B. James (Eds.), *Multiple Paths of Midlife Development* (pp. 1-17). Chicago, IL: University of Chicago Press.

Lachman, M. E., Lewkowicz, C., Marcus, A., & Peng, Y. (1994). Images of midlife development among young, middle-aged, and elderly adults. *Journal of Adult Development, 1*, 201-211.

LaGrange, R. L., & Ferraro, K. F. (1989). Assessing age and gender differences in perceived risk and fear of crime. *Criminology, 27*, 697-720.

Launer, L. J., & Harris, T. (1996). Weight, height and body mass index distributions in geographically and ethnically diverse samples of older persons. *Age and Ageing, 25*, 300-306.

Lawton, M. P. (1982). Competence, environmental press, and the adaptation of older people. In M. P. Lawton, P. G. Windley & T. O. Byerts (Eds.), *Aging and the Environment: Theoretical Approaches* (pp. 33-59). New York, NY: Springer Publishing Company.

Lawton, M. P., & Nahemow, L. (1973). Ecology and the aging process. In C. Eisdorfer & M. P. Lawton (Eds.), *The Psychology of Adult Development and Aging* (pp. 619-674). Washington, D.C.: American Psychological Association.

Lerner, R. M. (1993). Human development: A developmental contextual perspective. In S. C. Hayes, L. J. Hayes, H. W. Reese & T. R. Sarbin (Eds.), *Varieties of Scientific Contextualism* (pp. 301-315). Reno, NV: Context Press.

Leventhal, T., & Brooks-Gunn, J. (2000). The neighborhoods they live in: The effects of neighborhood residence on child and adolescent outcomes. *Psychological Bulletin, 126*, 309-337.

Li, F., Fisher, J., Brownson, R. C., & Bosworth, M. (2005). Multilevel modelling of built environment characteristics related to neighbourhood walking activity in older adults. *Journal of Epidemiology & Community Health, 59*, 558-564.

Lindstrom Johnson, S., Solomon, B. S., Shields, W. C., McDonald, E. M., McKenzie, L. B., & Gielen, A. C. (2009). Neighborhood violence and its association with mothers' health: Assessing the relative importance of perceived safety and exposure to violence. *Journal of Urban Health: Bulletin of the New York Academy of Medicine, 86*, 538-550.

Liska, A. E., & Warner, B. D. (1991). Functions of crime: A paradoxical process. *American Journal of Sociology, 96*, 1441-1463.

Macintyre, S., & Ellaway, A. (2000). Ecological approaches: Rediscovering the role of the physical and social environment. In L. F. Berkman & I. Kawachi (Eds.), *Social Epidemiology* (pp. 332-348). New York, NY: Oxford University Press.

Macintyre, S., Ellaway, A., & Cummins, S. (2002a). Place effects on health: How can we conceptualise, operationalise and measure them? *Social Science & Medicine, 55*, 125-139.

Macintyre, S., Ellaway, A., & Cummins, S. (2002b). Place effects on health: How can we conceptualise, operationalise and measure them? *Social Science and Medicine, 55*, 125-139.

Macintyre, S., MacIver, S., & Sooman, A. (1993). Area, class and health: Should we be focusing on places or people? *Journal of Social Policy, 22*, 213-234.

Maddux, J. E. (1995). Self-efficacy theory: An introduction. In J. E. Maddux (Ed.), *Self-efficacy, Adaptation, and Adjustment: Theory, Research, and Application* (pp. 3-33). New York, NY: Plenum Press.

Malmstrom, M., Sundquist, J., & Johansson, S. E. (1999). Neighborhood environment and self-reported health status: A multilevel analysis. *American Journal of Public Health, 89*, 1181-1186.

Marlatt, G. A., & Donovan, D. (2005). *Relapse Prevention* (2nd ed.). New York, NY: Guilford Press.

Maton, A. (1993). *Human Biology and Health*. Englewood Cliffs, NJ: Prentice Hall.

McDonald, K., & Thompson, J. K. (1992). Eating disturbance, body image dissatisfaction, and reasons for exercising: Gender differences and correlational findings. *International Journal of Eating Disorders, 11*, 289-292.

McGee, D. L., Liao, Y., Cao, G., & Cooper, R. S. (1999). Self-reported health status and mortality in a multiethnic US cohort. *American Journal of Epidemiology, 149*, 41-46.

McNeill, L. H., Wyrwich, K. W., Brownson, R. C., Clark, E. M., & Kreuter, M. W. (2006). Individual, social environmental, and physical environmental influences on physical activity among Black and White adults: A structural equation analysis. *Annals of Behavioral Medicine, 31*, 36-44.

Mendes de Leon, C. F., Cagney, K. A., Bienias, J. L., Barnes, L. L., Skarupski, K. A., Scherr, P. A., et al. (2009). Neighborhood social cohesion and disorder in relation to walking in community-dwelling older adults. *Journal of Aging and Health, 21*, 155-171.

Mensah, G. A., & Brown, D. W. (2007). An overview of cardiovascular disease burden in the United States. *Health Affairs, 26*, 38-48.

Merrill, S. S., & Verbruggee, L. M. (1999). Health and disease in midlife. In S. L. Willis & J. D. Reid (Eds.), *Life in the Middle: Psychological and Social Development in Middle Age* (pp. 78-103). San Diego, CA: Academic Press.

Miles, R. (2006). Neighborhood disorder and smoking: Findings of a European urban survey. *Social Science & Medicine, 63*, 2464-2475.

Mobley, L. R., Root, E. D., Finkelstein, E. A., Khavjou, O., Farris, R. P., & Will, J. C. (2006). Environment, obesity, and cardiovascular disease risk in low-income women. *American Journal of Preventive Medicine, 30*, 327-332.

Moen, P., & Wethington, E. (1999). Midlife development in a life course context. In S. L. Willis & J. D. Reid (Eds.), *Life in the Middle: Psychological and Social Development in Middle Age* (pp. 3-23). San Diego, CA: Academic Press.

Morris, K. S., McAuley, E., & Motl, R. W. (2008). Neighborhood satisfaction, functional limitations, and self-efficacy influences on physical activity in older women. *International Journal of Behavioral Nutrition and Physical Activity, 5*, 13-20.

Morrow Jr., J. R., Krzewinski-Malone, J. A., Jackson, A. W., Bungum, T. J., & FizGerald, S. J. (2004). American adults' knowledge of exercise recommendations. *Research Quarterly for Exercise and Sport, 75*, 231-237.

Mossey, J. M., & Shapiro, E. (1982). Self-rated health: A predictor of mortality among the elderly. *American Journal of Public Health, 72*, 800-808.

Nahemow, L. (2000). The ecological theory of aging: Powell Lawton's legacy. In R. L. Rubinstein, M. Moss & M. H. Kleban (Eds.), *The Many Dimensions of Aging* (pp. 22-40). New York, NY: Springer Publishing Company.

National Center for Health Statistics (2008). Prevalence of overweight, obesity and extreme obesity among adults: United States, trends 1960-62 through 2005-2006. Retrieved from http://www.cdc.gov/nchs/data/hestat/overweight/overweight_adult.htm

National Center for Health Statistics (2009). Health, United States, 2008 with Chartbook. Retrieved from http://www.cdc.gov/nchs/data/hus/hus08.pdf

Nelson, T. L., Brandon, D. T., Wiggins, S. A., & Whitfield, K. E. (2002). Genetic and environmental influences on body-fat measures among African-American twins. *Obesity Research, 10*, 733-739.

Neugarten, B. L. (Ed.). (1968). *Middle Age and Aging*. Chicago, IL: University of Chicago Press.

O'Hea, E. L., Boudreaux, E. D., Jeffries, S. K., Taylor, C. L. C., Scarinci, I. C., & Brantley, P. J. (2004). Stage of change movement across three health behaviors: The role of self-efficacy. *American Journal of Health Promotion, 19*, 94-102.

Ockene, J. K., Emmons, K. M., Mermelstein, R. J., Perkins, K. A., Bonollo, D. S., Voorhees, C. C., et al. (2000). Relapse and maintenance issues for smoking cessation. *Health Psychology, 19*(Suppl.), 17-31.

Office of the Chief Actuary (2009). Normal Retirement Age. Retrieved December 8, 2009: http://www.ssa.gov/OACT/ProgData/nra.html

Oh, J. (2003). Assessing the social bonds of elderly neighbors: The roles of length of residence, crime victimization, and perceived disorder. *Sociological Inquiry, 73*, 490-510.

Parkes, A., & Kearns, A. (2006). The multi-dimensional neighbourhood and health: A cross-sectional analysis of the Scottish Household Survey, 2001. *Health & Place, 12*, 1-18.

Pascarella, E. T., & Terenzini, P. T. (2005). *How College Affects Students. Volume 2: A Third Decade of Research*. San Francisco, CA: Jossey-Bass.

Pate, R. R., Pratt, M., Blair, S. N., Haskell, W. L., Macera, C. A., Bouchard, C., et al. (1995). Physical activity and public health. A recommendation from the Centers for Disease Control and Prevention and the American College of Sports Medicine. *Journal of the American Medical Association, 273*, 402-407.

Patterson, J. M., Eberly, L. E., Ding, Y., & Hargreaves, M. (2004). Associations of smoking prevalence with individual and area level social cohesion. *Journal of Epidemiology & Community Health, 58*, 692-697.

Perissinotto, E., Pisent, C., Sergi, G., Grigoletto, F., & Enzi, G. (2002). Anthropometric measurements in the elderly: Age and gender differences. *British Journal of Nutrition, 87*, 177-186.

Piro, F. N., Noess, O., & Claussen, B. (2006). Physical activity among elderly people in a city population: The influence of neighbourhood level violence and self perceived safety. *Journal of Epidemiology & Community Health, 60*, 626-632.

Pleis, J. R., & Lucas, J. W. (2009). Summary health statistics for U.S. adults: National Health Interview Survey, 2007 *Vital Health Stat* (Vol. 10 (no. 240)): National Center for Health Statistics.

Poortinga, W. (2006). Perceptions of the environment, physical activity, and obesity. *Social Science & Medicine, 63*, 2835-2846.

Raskind, M. A., Bonner, L. T., & Peskind, E. R. (2004). Cognitive disorders. In D. G. Blazer, D. C. Steffens & E. W. Busse (Eds.), *The American Psychiatric Publishing Textbook of Geriatric Psychiatry* (pp. 207-229). Arlington, VA: American Psychiatric Publishing, Inc.

Raudenbush, S. W. (2003). The quantitative assessment of neighborhood social environments. In I. Kawachi & L. F. Berkman (Eds.), *Neighborhoods and Health* (pp. 112-131). New York, NY: Oxford University Press.

Richman, L. S., Bennett, G. G., Pek, J., Siegler, I., & Williams Jr., R. B. (2007). Discrimination, dispositions, and cardiovascular responses to stress. *Health Psychology, 26*, 675-683.

Robert, S. A. (1998). Community-level socioeconomic status effects on adult health. *Journal of Health and Social Behavior, 39*, 18-37.

Robinson, J., & Godbey, G. (1997). *The Surprising Ways Americans Use Their Time*. University Park, PA: Pennsylvania State University Press.

Rosenbaum, E., & Harris, L. E. (2001). Low-income families in their new neighborhoods. *Journal of Family Issues, 22*, 183-210.

Ross, C. E. (1993). Fear of victimization and health. *Journal of Quantitative Criminology, 9*, 159-175.

Ross, C. E. (2000). Walking, exercising, and smoking: Does neighborhood matter? *Social Science & Medicine, 51*, 265-274.

Ross, C. E., & Mirowsky, J. (1999). Disorder and decay: The concept and measurement of perceived neighborhood disorder. *Urban Affairs Quarterly, 34*, 412-432.

Rubinstein, R. L. (1989). The home environments of older people: A description of the psychosocial processes linking person to place. *Journal of Gerontology: Social Sciences, 44*, S45-S53.

Rutter, M., Dunn, J., Plomin, R., Simonoff, E., Pickles, A., Maughan, B., et al. (1997). Integrating nature and nurture: Implications of person-environment correlations and interactions for developmental psychopathology. *Development and Psychopathology, 9*, 335-364.

Ryff, C. D., & Seltzer, M. M. (Eds.). (1996). *The Parental Experience in Midlife*. Chicago, IL: The University of Chicago Press

Sallis, J. F., Hovell, M. F., & Hofstetter, C. R. (1992). Predictors of adoption of maitenance of vigorous physical activity in men and women. *Preventive Medicine, 21*, 237-251.

Sampson, R. J., Morenoff, J. D., & Earls, F. (1999). Beyond social capital: Spatial dynamics of collective efficacy for children. *American Sociological Review, 65*, 633-659.

Sampson, R. J., & Raudenbush, S. W. (1999). Systematic social observation of public spaces: A new look at disorder in urban neighborhoods. *American Journal of Sociology, 105*, 603-651.

Sampson, R. J., Raudenbush, S. W., & Earls, F. (1997). Neighborhoods and violent crime: A multilevel study of collective efficacy. *Science, 277*, 918-924.

Satariano, W. A., Haight, T. J., & Tager, I. B. (2000). Reasons given by older people for limitation or avoidance of leisure time physical activity. *Journal of the American Geriatrics Society, 48*, 505-512.

Satorra, A., & Bentler, P. M. (1994). Corrections to test statistic and standard errors in covariance structure analysis. In A. Von Eye & C. C. Clogg (Eds.), *Analysis of Latent Variables in Developmental Research* (pp. 399-419). Newbury Park, CA: Sage Publications.

Schwarzer, R., & Fuchs, R. (1996). Self-efficacy and health behaviours. In M. Conner & P. Norman (Eds.), *Predicting Health Behaviour: Research and Practice with Social Cognition Models* (pp. 163-196). Bristol, PA: Open University Press.

Schwesinger, G. C. (1933). *Heredity and Environment*. New York, NY: Macmillan.

Settersten Jr., R. A. (2006). Aging and the life course. In R. H. Binstock & L. K. George (Eds.), *Handbook of Aging and the Social Sciences* (6th ed., pp. 3-19). San Diego, CA: Academic Press.

Shenassa, E. D., Liebhaber, A., & Ezeamama, A. (2006). Perceived safety of area of residence and exercise: A pan-European study. *American Journal of Epidemiology, 163*, 1012-1017.

Shenk, D., Kuwahara, K., & Zablotsky, D. (2004). Older women's attachments to their home and possessions. *Journal of Aging Studies, 18*, 157-169.

Shephard, R. J. (1998). Aging and exercise. *Encyclopedia of Sports Medicine and Science*. Retrieved from http://www.sportsci.org/encyc/agingex/agingex.html

Silberstein, L. R., Striegel-Moore, R. H., Timko, C., & Rodin, J. (1988). Behavioral and psychological implications of body dissatisfaction: Do men and women differ? *Sex Roles, 19*, 219-232.

Skogan, W. G. (1990). *Disorder and decline: Crime and spiral decay in American neighborhoods*. New York, NY: The Free Press.

Snelgrove, J. W., Pikhart, H., & Stafford, M. (2009). A multilevel analysis of social capital and self-rated health: Evidence from the British Household Panel Survey. *Social Science & Medicine, 68*, 1993-2001.

Social Security Online (2009). The Full Retirement Age is Increasing. Retrieved December 8, 2009: http://www.ssa.gov/pubs/ageincrease.htm

Stack, C. (1996). *Call to Home: African Americans Claim the Rural South*. New York, NY: Basic Books.

Stark Casagrande, S., Whitt-Glover, M. C., Lancaster, K. J., Odoms-Young, A. M., & Gary, T. L. (2009). Built environment and health behaviors among African Americans: A systematic review. *American Journal of Preventive Medicine, 36*, 174-181.

Steiger, J. H. (1990). Structural model evaluation and modification: An interval estimation approach. *Multivariate Behavioral Research, 25*, 173-180.

Steiger, J. H., & Lind, J. C. (1980). *Statistically based tests for the number of factors*. Paper presented at the annual spring meeting of the Psychometric Society.

Stein, C. J., & Colditz, G. A. (2004). Modifiable risk factors for cancer. *British Journal of Cancer, 90*, 299-303.

Steptoe, A., & Wardle, J. (2004). Health-related behaviour: Prevalence and links with disease. In A. Kaptein & J. Weinman (Eds.), *Health Psychology* (pp. 21-51). Malden, MA: Blackwell Publishing.

Suminski, R. R., Carlos Poston, W. S., Petosa, R. L., Stevens, E., & Katzenmoyer, L. M. (2005). Features of the neighborhood environment and walking by U.S. adults. *American Journal of Preventive Medicine, 28,* 149-155.

Sundquist, K., Theobald, H., Yang, M., Li, X., Johansson, S., & Sundquist, J. (2006). Neighborhood violent crime and unemployment increase the risk of coronary heart disease: A multilevel study in an urban setting. *Social Science & Medicine, 62,* 2061-2071.

Tanner, J., & Yabiku, S. (1999). Conclusion: The economics of young adulthood- One future or two? In A. Booth, A. Crouter & M. Shanahan (Eds.), *Transitions to Adulthood in a Changing Economy: No Work, No Family, No Future?* (pp. 254-268). Westport, CT: Praeger.

Taylor, R. B. (1996). Neighborhood responses to disorder and local attachments: The systematic model of attachment, social disorganization, and neighborhood use value. *Sociological Forum, 11,* 41-74.

Taylor, S. E., Repetti, R. L., & Seeman, T. (1997). Health Psychology: What is an unhealthy environment and how does it get under the skin? *Annual Review of Psychology, 48,* 441-447.

Tiggemann, M., & Williamson, S. (2000). The effect of exercise on body satisfaction and self-esteem as a function of gender and age. *Sex Roles, 43,* 119-127.

Tomarken, A. J., & Waller, N. G. (2005). Structural equation modeling: Strengths, limitations, and misconceptions. *Annual Review of Clinical Psychology, 1,* 31-65.

Troped, P. J., Saunders, R. P., Pate, R. R., Reininger, B., & Addy, C. L. (2003). Correlates of recreational and transportation physical activity among adults in a New England community. *Preventive Medicine, 37,* 304-310.

Tucker-Seeley, R. D., Subramanian, S. V., Li, Y., & Sorensen, G. (2009). Neighborhood safety, socioeconomic status, and physical activity in older adults. *American Journal of Preventive Medicine, 37,* 207-213.

Tucker, L. R., & Lewis, C. (1973). A reliability coefficient for maximum likelihood factor analysis. *Psychometrika, 38,* 1-10.

U.S. Department of Health and Human Services (1996). *Physical Activity and Health: A Report of the Surgeon General*. Atlanta, GA: U.S. Department of Health and

Human Services, Centers for Disease Control and Prevention, National Center for Chronic Disease Prevention and Health Promotion.

United States Census Bureau (2006). *Oldest Baby Boomers Turn 60!* Retrieved from http://www.census.gov/Press-Release/www/releases/archives/facts_for_features_special_editions/006105.html

Veenstra, G. (2000). Social capital, SES and health: An individual-level analysis. *Social Science & Medicine, 50*, 619-629.

Wane, S., van Uffelen, J. G. Z., & Brown, W. (2010). Determinants of weight gain in young women: A review of the literature. *Journal of Women's Health, 19*, 1327-1340.

Weden, M. M., Carpiano, R. M., & Robert, S. A. (2008). Subjective and objective neighborhood characteristics and adult health. *Social Science & Medicine, 66*, 1256-1270.

Wen, M., Hawkley, L. C., & Cacioppo, J. T. (2006). Objective and perceived neighborhood environment, individual SES and psychosocial factors and self-rated health: An analysis of older adults in Cook County, Illinois. *Social Science & Medicine, 63*, 2575-2590.

Wen, M., Kandula, N. R., & Lauderdale, D. S. (2007). Walking for transportation or leisure: What difference does the neighborhood make? *Journal of General Internal Medicine, 22*, 1674-1680.

White, G. E. (2001). Home ownership: Crime and the tipping and trapping processes. *Environment and Behavior, 33*, 325-342.

Whitfield, K. E., Weidner, G., Clark, R., & Anderson, N. B. (2002). Sociodemographic diversity and behavioral medicine. *Journal of Consulting and Clinical Psychology, 70*, 463-481.

Wilbur, J., Chandler, P. J., Dancy, B., & Lee, H. (2003). Correlates of physical activity in urban midwestern African-American women. *American Journal of Preventive Medicine, 25*, 45-52.

Wilcox, S., Bopp, M., Oberrecht, L., Kammermann, S. K., & McElmurray, C. T. (2003). Psychosocial and perceived environmental correlates of physical activity in rural older African American and White women. *Journal of Gerontology, 58B*, P329-P337.

Willems, S., De Maesschalck, S., Deveugele, M., Derese, A., & De Maeseneer, J. (2005). Socio-economic status of the patient and doctor-patient communication: Does it make a difference? *Patient Education & Counseling, 56*, 139-146.

Williams, D. R., & Mohammed, S. A. (2009). Discrimination and racial disparities in health: Evidence and needed research. *Journal of Behavioral Medicine, 32*, 20-47.

Williamson, D. F., Madans, J., Anda, R. F., Kleinman, J. C., Giovino, G. A., & Byers, T. (1991). Smoking cessation and severity of weight gain in a national cohort. *New England Journal of Medicine, 324*, 739-745.

Willis, S. L., & Martin, M. (Eds.). (2005). *Middle Adulthood: A Lifespan Perspective*. Thousand Oaks, CA: Sage Publications.

Willis, S. L., & Reid, J. D. (Eds.). (1999). *Life in the Middle: Psychological and Social Development in Middle Age*. San Diego, CA: Academic Press.

Biography

Lea R. Bromell

Born February 25, 1982 in Worcester, Massachusetts.

Education

M.A. 2009 Duke University, Durham, NC
             Developmental Psychology

B.A. 2004 Duke University, Durham, NC
             Major: Psychology (Certificate: Human Development)

Publications

Bromell, L., & Whitfield, K.E. (in prep). Education, stress, and health among African American adults: A comparison of two age groups.

Burton, L.M., & **Bromell, L.** (2010). Childhood illness, family co-morbidity, and cumulative disadvantage: An ethnographic treatise on low-income mothers' health in later life. *Annual Review of Gerontology and Geriatrics, 30*, 233-265.

Whitfield, K.E., **Bromell, L.**, Bennett, G., & Edwards, C.L. (2009). Biobehavioral perspectives on health morbidities in late life. *Annual Review of Gerontology and Geriatrics, 29*, 57-76.

Hill, N.E., Tyson, D.F., & **Bromell, L**. (2009). Developmentally appropriate strategies across ethnicity and socio-economic status: Parental involvement during middle school. In N. E. Hill & R. K. Chao (Eds.), *Families, Schools, and the Adolescent: Connecting Research, Policy, and Practice*. NY: Teachers College Press.

Hill, N.E., **Bromell, L.**, Tyson, D.F., & Flint, R.C. (2007). Ecological perspectives on parental influences during adolescence. *Journal of Clinical Child and Adolescent Psychology, 36*, 367-377.

Awards

Summer 2010 Leadership in an Aging Society Fellowship, Center for the Study of Aging and Human Development, Duke University

2009-2010 E. Bayard Halsted Fellowship, The Graduate School, Duke University

2005- 2009 Duke Endowment Fellowship, The Graduate School, Duke University

CPSIA information can be obtained
at www.ICGtesting.com
Printed in the USA
LVIW021557061212

310442LV00005B

9 781249 042440